Many Gifts

Series Advisor
Fr. Michael T. Ryan

Series Authors
Mary Cairo
Luci Soncin

Series Consultant
Jennette MacKenzie

Social Studies Consultant
Angelo Bolotta

1914–2014: Nelson Education celebrates 100 years of Canadian publishing

NELSON EDUCATION

Many Gifts 5 Student Book

Series Advisor
Fr. Michael T. Ryan

Series Authors
Mary Cairo
Luci Soncin

Series Consultant
Jennette MacKenzie

Social Studies Consultant
Angelo Bolotta

Executive Publisher
Lara Caplan

Managing Editor
Alexandra Romic

Senior Editor
Diane Robitaille

Product Manager
Jessie MacKinnon

Program Manager
Jackie Brown

Developmental Editors
Kelly Cochrane
Su Mei Ku
Jennifer Stanicak

Editorial Assistant
Jackie Marchildon

Director, Content and Media Production
Carol Martin

Senior Production Project Manager
Jane High

Senior Content Production Editor
Jane High

Copyeditor
Linda Szostak

Proofreader
Cathy Fraccaro

Design Director
Ken Phipps

Interior Design
Trinh Truong

Cover Design
Trinh Truong

Cover Images
(main photo)
Jupiterimages/Thinkstock
(photo bottom left)
Rolf Hicker Photography/Alamy
(photo bottom centre)
Pantheon/Superstock
(photo bottom right)
North Wind Picture Archives/Alamy

Asset Coordinator
Suzanne Peden

Illustrators
Michael Borop
Crowle Art
Ted Hammond

Compositors
Barb Kelly
Jennifer Leung
Kathy Mo
Trinh Truong

Photo Shoot Coordinator
Christine Elliott

Photo/Permissions Researcher
Indu Arora

COPYRIGHT © 2014 by Nelson Education Ltd.

ISBN-13: 978-0-17-65306-0
ISBN-10: 0-17-653060-6

Printed and bound in Canada
1 2 3 4 17 16 15 14

For more information contact Nelson Education Ltd., 1120 Birchmount Road, Toronto, Ontario M1K 5G4. Or you can visit our website at www.nelson.com.

Excerpts from this publication may be reproduced under licence from Access Copyright, or with the express written permission of Nelson Education Ltd., or as permitted by law. Requests which fall outside of Access Copyright guidelines must be submitted online to www.cengage.com/permissions. Further questions about permissions can be emailed to permissionrequest@cengage.com.

ALL RIGHTS ARE OTHERWISE RESERVED. No part of this publication may be reproduced, stored in a retrieval system, or transmitted in any form or by any means, electronic, mechanic, photocopying, scanning, recording or otherwise, except as specifically authorized.

Every effort has been made to trace ownership of all copyrighted material and to secure permission from copyright holders. In the event of any question arising as to the use of any material, we will be pleased to make the necessary corrections in future printings.

Advisory Panel

Patricia Amos
Michael Bator
Fran Craig
Martha Dutrizak
Aimee Gerdevich
Anne Jamieson
Lorne Keon
Bronek Korczynski
John Kostoff
Dr. Josephine Lombardi
Patricia Manson
Noel Martin
Sharron McKeever
Jim Minello
Susan Perry
Lou Rocha
Suzanne Wishak

Nelson would like to offer special thanks to Sr. Joan Cronin, g.s.i.c., for her guidance and advice.

Series Consultants and Contributors

Mary Bender, Assessment Contributor
Michael Borop, Cartography Reviewer
Wilfred Burton, Aboriginal Reviewer
Nancy Christoffer, Bias Reviewer
Fran Craig, Assessment Contributor
Lynnita-Jo Guillet, Aboriginal Reviewer
Ovey Mohammed, s.j., Professor, Theology Reviewer
Byron Moldofsky, Cartography Reviewer
Dyanne Rivers, Social Studies Reviewer
Rachel Urowitz, Professor, Religious History Reviewer

Series Reviewers

Antoinette Armenti-Lambert, *Niagara CDSB*
Mariella Bruni, *Dufferin–Peel CDSB*
Betty Brush, *Windsor–Essex CDSB*
Lori Bryden, *Algonquin and Lakeshore CDSB*
Michelle Bryden, *CDSB of Eastern Ontario*
Monica Campbell, *London DCSB*
Erin Cassone, *Huron–Perth CDSB*
Alan Creelman, *Niagara CDSB*
Nancy Das Neves, *Toronto CDSB*
Marina DiGirolamo, *York CDSB*
Shawn Evon, *Dufferin–Peel CDSB*
Vania Grober, *Toronto CDSB*
Julia Janveau, *Nipissing–Parry Sound CDSB*
Deborah Karam, *Toronto CDSB*
Vivian Ku, *York CDSB*
Anne Marie Maloney, *Niagara CDSB*
Yvonne Minard, *Durham CDSB*
Susan Nelan, *Hamilton–Wentworth CDSB*
Susanne Nolan, *Nipissing–Parry Sound CDSB*
Terri Pauco, *Niagara CDSB*
Michelle Peres, *Toronto CDSB*
Deanna Perry, *Ottawa CSB*
Ralph Peter, *Toronto CDSB*
Lino Pin, *Hamilton–Wentworth CDSB*
Carmelina Pinozzotto, *Niagara CDSB*
Grant Ranalli, *Hamilton–Wentworth CDSB*
Daniel Reidy, *Dufferin–Peel CDSB*
Lynne Ruetz, *Durham CDSB*
Sandra Scime, *Hamilton–Wentworth CDSB*
Alan Skeoch, Retired, *Toronto DSB*
Jillian Stefik, *Durham CDSB*
Seán Stokes, *St. Michael's College School*
William Swartz, Retired, *Toronto DSB*
David Tignanelli, *Nipissing–Parry Sound CDSB*
Carol Vaage, *Edmonton CSD*
Josie Zuppa, *Hamilton–Wentworth CDSB*

Contributing Writers

Andrea Bishop
Maureen Keenan

Contents *Many Gifts 5*

Why Do You Learn Social Studies?   4

Exploring *Many Gifts 5*   8

Unit 1 Canadian Government and Citizenship   10

Chapter 1	Local Government	16
Chapter 2	Provincial and Territorial Governments	36
Chapter 3	Federal Government	54
Chapter 4	Working Together	72
Chapter 5	The Rights and Responsibilities of Canadians	86
Unit Inquiry	An Action Plan for the Common Good	102

Unit 2 First Nations and European Explorers 106

Chapter 6	First Nations Peoples in Eastern Canada	112
Chapter 7	Early Contact	134
Chapter 8	Fur Trade in Eastern Canada	156
Chapter 9	Early Settlements in New France	178
Unit Inquiry	Investigating First Nations Peoples and Europeans in Early Canada	200
Glossary		204
Index		208

Why Do You Learn Social Studies?

The simplest answer to this question is: You learn social studies to become a better member of your community. When you learn about Canada and the world, you take the first steps on the road to becoming a responsible, active citizen. You become more thoughtful and knowledgeable and learn to value the differences and similarities people share.

You also develop the skills to

- use tools to gather and analyze information, solve problems, and communicate
- investigate issues and events
- evaluate information and evidence and make judgments
- build relationships

Active Participation
Work for the common good in local, national, and global communities.

Identity
Develop a sense of personal identity as a member of various communities.

Structures
Understand how communities are structured.

Attributes
Demonstrate positive character traits, values, and habits of mind.

What Does Being an Active Citizen Mean?

Being an active citizen means you will

- work for the common good
- develop a sense of yourself as part of a community
- understand how communities are structured
- develop positive character traits and values

What Are You Going to Learn?

This resource is divided into two units. The first unit is called **Canadian Government and Citizenship**. In this unit, you will learn about Canada's systems of government and about being an active citizen. You'll also acquire some mapping and inquiry skills that will help you learn.

The second unit is called **First Nations and European Explorers**. In this unit, you'll learn about some of the First Nations peoples who lived in Canada before it was even a country. You will also learn about the European explorers who came to this country long ago. You will investigate the interactions between First Nations peoples and explorers, fur traders, and settlers. You will discover how the environment affected each group, and how each group affected the environment. As well, you will reflect on how this history affects us today.

How Are You Going to Learn?

Throughout this resource, you will acquire the skills to help you learn by using the inquiry process. The inquiry process can help you investigate, solve problems, and reach conclusions. The inquiry process has five components:

- formulate questions
- gather and organize information, evidence, and data
- interpret and analyze information, evidence, and data
- evaluate information, evidence, and data and then draw conclusions
- communicate what you discover

It's important to remember that you may not use all of these components during every inquiry or investigation. For example, sometimes, your teacher will give you the inquiry question. Sometimes, you may not have to communicate what you discover.

The Inquiry Process

- Formulate Questions
- Gather and Organize
- Interpret and Analyze
- Evaluate and Draw Conclusions
- Communicate

The Social Studies Thinking Concepts

Being a successful learner in social studies is not just about remembering facts, such as how many provinces and territories Canada has. To be a successful learner, you are also going to need the following thinking concepts. These **thinking concepts** give you ways to look at and evaluate information.

When You Think about …	You Need to …	Sample Questions You Might Ask
Significance	Determine the importance of something (for example, an event, issue, person, or place). Often, the significance of something depends on the situation or the people involved.	Why is this event important now? Why was this event important long ago? Was this event important to everyone?
Cause and Consequence	Identify and examine the factors that lead up to an event, as well as the impact of that event.	What caused this event to happen? Who was affected? How were they affected? What happened next?
Continuity and Change	Identify what has stayed the same and what has changed over a period of time. You will compare two points in the past or compare the past with the present.	How is this early time period different from our own? How are they the same? What causes them to be different or the same? What can we learn from comparing these two time periods?
Patterns and Trends	Make connections to identify characteristics or traits that are repeated over a period of time or in different locations.	How does what happened there/then connect with what happened here/now? What do these things have in common?
Interrelationships	Explore the relationships within and between societies, peoples, and/or systems.	How are these things related? What interactions do they have? How do they work together? What causes conflict? How is conflict resolved?
Perspective	Consider how different people or groups might view something, based on their beliefs, social position, location, and so on. You also need to consider how the sources you use during an inquiry have a particular perspective.	Who is giving us this information? What is their perspective? Is it the same as your perspective?

Sometimes, you will notice that these thinking concepts overlap. For example, when you are thinking about the significance of an event, it may be from a particular perspective. When you are thinking about how societies are related, you may also be thinking about the cause and consequence of particular events.

The Social Justice Teachings

You also bring to your social studies learning an understanding of Catholic teachings. The following six teachings should guide your thinking about social studies. As well, as you read the *Many Gifts 5* Student Book, Father Mike appears at the beginning of each unit and the end of every chapter to help you understand what you are learning from a Catholic perspective.

When You Think about the Social Justice Teaching of …	You Need to Understand That …	Sample Questions for Reflection in Social Studies
The Dignity of the Human Person	Humans are special because we can know and love God. We honour God by caring for one another and for God's world.	How did people care for and respect one another? How did this show they were honouring God?
The Person as Part of a Family and a Community	To be human is to be part of a group of people, whether a family or a community. These groups help make us who we are.	What goals did people share? How did they work together?
The Person's Role in the Common Good	The larger groups to which we belong help us to do things we could never do alone. In return, we need to follow the rules and make sacrifices to keep the groups strong.	What did people do to help one another?
The Person's Rights and Responsibilities	We all have responsibilities within our communities; we also have rights—to food, shelter, education, and so on.	What rights and responsibilities did people have?
The Person's Special Responsibility to the Poor and Vulnerable	We serve God by being good to those in need or to those who are suffering.	How did people care for one another, especially those in need or suffering?
The Person as God's Manager, Worker, and Steward of Creation	We are God's assistants in caring for the world so it will be a good home for us and safe for the people who come after us.	How did people act as stewards of Creation? How did they respect the gifts God gave us?

Exploring Many Gifts 5

This book will be your guide to the exciting world of social studies. Here are some of the features you will see.

The **Unit Opener** introduces the unit. Use the title, introductory paragraph, and opening map to predict what you will discover in the unit.

The **Our Faith** quotation provides a Catholic perspective for each unit.

The **Big Ideas** are questions you will be reflecting on throughout the unit.

Father Mike Explains ... presents the Catholic Social Justice Teaching for the unit.

Looking Ahead to the Unit Inquiry prepares you for the Unit Inquiry task at the end of the unit.

The **Big Question** is the guiding question for each chapter.

The **Learning Goals** tell you what you will learn in the chapter.

Headings introduce new topics. New vocabulary words appear in bold.

Photos and other images and their captions provide more information and opportunities to explore a topic.

Each **Catholic Connection** provides an opportunity to link the social studies topics to the Catholic faith.

Each section ends with some questions for reflection, as well as an opportunity to apply your learning.

8 Exploring Many Gifts

Each chapter includes a **Toolbox** that focuses on the inquiry process and other skills connected to social studies.

Opportunities to focus on the six social studies thinking concepts are provided in the **Thinking about ...** feature.

At the end of each chapter, there are many opportunities to reflect on and show your learning in **Pulling It Together**.

The **Chapter Inquiry** task will help prepare you for the Unit Inquiry task at the end of each unit.

The **Unit Inquiry** guides you through the five steps of the inquiry process as you investigate an issue or challenge that interests you.

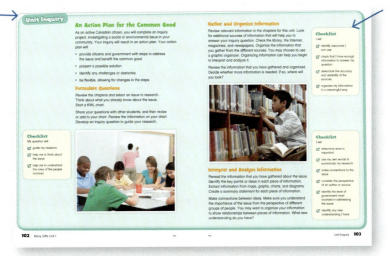

Checklists help remind you what to do at each stage of the process.

Exploring Many Gifts

Unit 1
Canadian Government and Citizenship

Canada has different levels of government. In this unit, you will learn about these different levels. You will also learn about ways in which Canadian citizens of all ages can participate in government. You will be invited to become an active citizen. By accepting this invitation, you will learn how to make your voice heard. You will be encouraged to serve your community, the environment, and the common good.

This diamond mine near Yellowknife is overseen by the territorial government.

Citizens gather in Kitimat, British Columbia, to protest a proposed oil and gas pipeline.

Light rail transit in Edmonton is the responsibility of local government.

Our Faith

The Prayer of St. Francis says ...

"Lord, make me an instrument of your peace. Where there is hatred, let me sow love; where there is injury, pardon; where there is doubt, faith; where there is despair, hope; where there is darkness, light; where there is sadness, joy."

10 Many Gifts Unit 1

Political Map of Canada

Big Ideas
- How do the different levels of government serve citizens?
- How do governments work together to serve the common good?
- What are the rights and responsibilities of Canadians?

Patrolling Arctic waters is a federal responsibility.

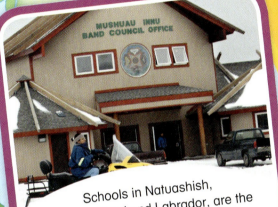
Schools in Natuashish, Newfoundland and Labrador, are the responsibility of the band council.

Fighting this forest fire near Thunder Bay, Ontario, is the responsibility of different levels of government.

Legend
- ★ national capital
- ● province/territory capital
- ▬ international boundary
- ― province/territory boundary

Canadian Government and Citizenship

What Is Government?

The word **government** refers to a group of citizens who have been elected to provide leadership. The government makes decisions and passes laws to meet the needs of the people it serves and represents. There are different levels of government in Canada. The different levels of government make sure that everyone's basic needs are met.

Level of Government	Responsibilities
Local	looks after issues in a community or local area
Provincial/Territorial	looks after issues that affect a province or territory
Federal	looks after issues that affect the entire country

Aboriginal peoples also have levels of government, which work alongside other governments in Canada.

Level of Government	Responsibilities
Local	looks after issues in First Nations, Inuit, and Métis communities
Provincial/Territorial Organizations, Tribal Councils	serve the needs of more than one community in a province, territory, or region
National Organizations	look after issues that affect Aboriginal peoples across Canada

This photo shows the Métis National Council president, Clément Chartier, speaking to Métis war veterans in 2009.

This photo shows the Parliament buildings. Canada's federal government meets in Ottawa, Ontario, within these buildings.

Government is involved in all aspects of daily life, from taking care of local parks to providing healthcare to defending our borders. A different level of government is responsible for each of these services.

Active citizens stay informed about issues and challenges in their communities. They help elect leaders they can trust to work toward solutions. Active citizens also take part in activities that make the community a better place for all to live.

Catholic Connection

Social justice is an important part of the teachings of the Church. Governments play a large role in social justice by creating communities that treat all members with dignity and respect.

Active citizens work to make our communities better and to protect our environment. Would you describe yourself as an active citizen? Why, or why not?

Canadian Government and Citizenship

Getting Started

Before learning about something new, it is important to think about what you already know. Then, you can formulate questions about what you want to discover. Here are some questions and thoughts that Nicole had about citizenship and government.

My Questions and Thoughts

- Why do we need different levels of government? Do the different levels work together? Who runs hospitals and schools?

- How do people resolve an issue or problem in their community? I think voting is one way we can communicate with the government. What other ways are there?

- Canada has lots of different people who have different needs. I wonder how we make sure that all Canadians are represented. How are the needs of so many different people met?

- I know I have a right to an education. I wonder what other rights I have. How are our rights protected? Does everyone in Canada have the same rights?

Explore and Apply

1. What do you already know about government and citizenship?

2. Generate your own list of questions about government and citizenship. Look for answers to your questions as you read this unit.

Father Mike Explains ...

Life is not just about me; it is about us. Humans are made in the image of God, and God is a divine society of three Persons—Father, Son, and Holy Spirit—whose life is one of perfect unity and total love. So, we are not just individuals. To be human is to be part of various societies and communities that help make us who we are.

When we study the various forms of government, we are looking at the ways we have chosen to organize life together so that we can pursue the common good. To have good societies, we need good governments to make good laws and provide good services. To have good governments, we need people who are active in their communities and who are thoughtful when choosing those who govern us.

Looking Ahead to the Unit Inquiry

For the unit inquiry, you will investigate an issue in your community and draw conclusions about how to resolve it. You will then create a plan of action to bring this issue to the attention of others.

Using your knowledge of government and active citizenship, you will

- identify an issue
- create an action plan that contributes to a solution
- identify the level of government most involved in addressing your issue

See pages 102 to 105 for more information on the Unit Inquiry.

Chapter 1

Local Government

Big Question

What decisions do local governments make that support the common good?

Learning Goals

- explain why different groups may have different perspectives on social and environmental issues
- formulate questions about an issue
- assess the effectiveness of actions taken by local governments

This aerial photo shows the Red Hill Valley Parkway in Hamilton

Hi, I'm Alex.

I live in Hamilton, Ontario. Hamilton is a busy city with a lot of traffic. My mom works on the other side of the city from where we live. It used to take her an hour to get home. She says the drive is a lot better now that the city built the Red Hill Valley Parkway. That's a highway near our house.

My mom said that she was against building the highway at first. She thought that the project would cost too much money and that it would destroy natural areas by the creek. Other people agreed with her. In fact, some people were so concerned that they camped by Red Hill Creek and blocked workers who came to build the road.

I wonder how a city can go ahead if not everyone agrees with a decision. How does a city make fair decisions?

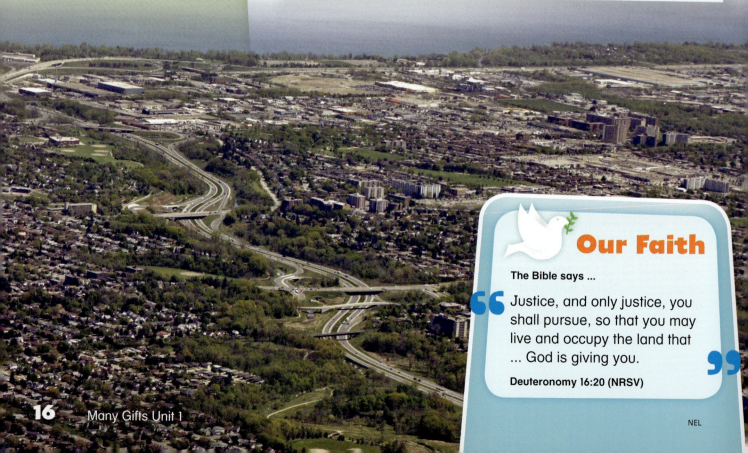

Our Faith

The Bible says ...

"Justice, and only justice, you shall pursue, so that you may live and occupy the land that ... God is giving you."

Deuteronomy 16:20 (NRSV)

What Is Local Government?

A **local government** is a group of people who are elected to make decisions for a town, city, village, or small region. Local governments make local laws. They also provide local services, such as picking up garbage and looking after local parks.

The power to make decisions and laws for an area is called **jurisdiction**. A local government has jurisdiction over the community it serves. Its decisions apply only to that community. Local governments cannot make decisions or laws that go against those made by higher levels of government. For example, Canadian law says that every citizen who is 18 or older can vote. A local government cannot pass a law that changes this age to 21.

Local governments make decisions about what activities are allowed in certain areas. They also make traffic bylaws to keep people safe.

Local governments often deal with issues that are unique to their communities. For example, in Banff, Alberta, local officials had to deal with a large number of elk that moved into the town. What special issues does your community deal with?

Thinking about Perspective

Banff, Alberta, has become home to a large number of elk. Many of the townspeople don't like the elk because they eat their grass. However, tourists in Banff like seeing the elk. What other perspectives on the elk might there be? For example, how do you think the mayor or local store owners might feel?

Municipalities

The most common type of local government is municipal government. A municipality can be an urban area, a rural area, or a mix of both. Cities, towns, townships, and villages are the most common types of municipalities.

Municipalities are created by the provincial or territorial government. Municipalities are created because the provincial or territorial government is not close enough to local issues to understand them and make decisions.

Municipal Government

A **municipality** is a community or an area that has its own local government. This type of local government is called **municipal government**. **Regional municipalities** are regions that include more than one municipality. Each municipality has its own government to deal with its own issues. However, the municipalities can come together to deal with larger issues or to share the cost of providing services.

Municipalities vary widely in size. These photos show two very different municipalities in Ontario, the city of Windsor (right) and the town of Killarney (below). Compare these two communities.

Local government works closely with the provincial or territorial government. Much of the money that municipal governments need comes from the provincial or territorial government. For this reason, municipal governments have to report to the provincial or territorial government. It also means that the province or territory can influence decisions that municipal governments make.

Map of the Regional Municipality of York

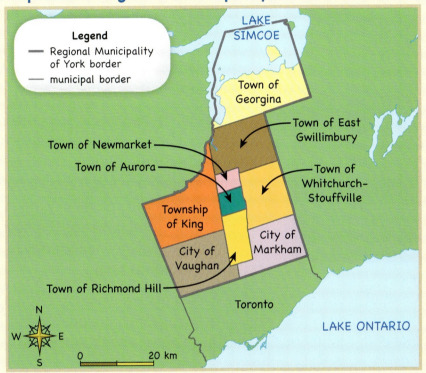

This is the crest, or badge, for York Regional Police. This police force watches over all municipalities in York Region. This means that each municipality does not have to create a police force of its own. What do you think each symbol on this crest suggests about this region?

The Regional Municipality of York is made up of nine municipalities. Each municipality is responsible for collecting its own garbage. However, the municipalities share the cost of building and running waste processing stations. This is much less expensive than building processing stations for each municipality.

Explore and Apply

1. Explain why it is important for a community to have the ability to make laws and provide the services that it needs.

2. Think about how you could organize information about each level of government: local, provincial/territorial, and federal. Start a graphic organizer with what you have learned so far. Add to the graphic organizer as you learn more about each level.

How Is Municipal Government Structured?

Every municipal government is made up of different groups of people. These groups include councils, boards, departments, and committees.

Municipal Councils

A **municipal council** is a group of people who have been elected to make decisions for a municipality. The elected members of the council are called **councillors**.

The community also elects one person to lead the council. This person is called the **head of council**. In a large centre, the head of council is called a **mayor**. In a smaller community, he or she might be called a **reeve**. The head of council in a regional municipality is called the **regional chair**.

The size of a local council depends on the number of people in the community. For example, this photo shows Toronto's city council, which has 44 councillors and a mayor. The town of Moosonee, Ontario, has a mayor and four councillors.

Municipal councils must meet at least once a month to discuss local issues and make plans. These meetings are open to community members. Community members can listen and present any ideas or concerns that they have.

Elected Officials on Local Councils

Position	How Many?	Some Responsibilities
Head of Council	• one person	• represents the municipality or regional municipality in discussions with other levels of government • leads council meetings • ensures that decisions made by council are put into action
Councillors	• number depends on the size of the community	• attend council meetings to speak for the area they represent • take part in small groups, called committees, that consider specific issues • make decisions based on the needs of the people they represent by voting for or against different projects presented in council meetings • inform people about decisions made by council

20 Many Gifts Unit 1

Boards, Commissions, and Committees

Boards and commissions are made up of groups of people who help municipal governments manage services and make decisions. These groups are responsible for watching over particular services. For example, a transit commission is responsible for issues related to public transportation. Members of boards and commissions meet regularly to discuss different issues related to their service.

Standing committees operate very much like boards and commissions. For example, there may be a standing committee that discusses issues around community arts and culture. Another type of committee, called a special committee, is created to study a single issue or project, such as building a bridge.

Municipal Departments

Municipal departments are made up of people who have knowledge and skills in a particular area. Every department has one person who leads it, called a **department head** (or chief). For example, the fire chief is the head of the fire department. The council often asks the department head for information about his or her department, or asks for his or her help when making decisions.

Municipal libraries are usually managed by a library board that reports to the municipal council. The library board decides what library resources and programs will suit the community's needs.

Below is an example of how a municipal government might be structured. The figure includes some common municipal departments. It also shows the city manager, who helps the council communicate with the department heads.

Sample Municipal Government Structure

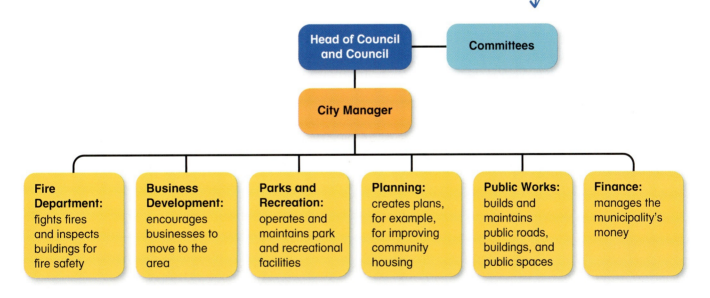

Fire Department: fights fires and inspects buildings for fire safety

Business Development: encourages businesses to move to the area

Parks and Recreation: operates and maintains park and recreational facilities

Planning: creates plans, for example, for improving community housing

Public Works: builds and maintains public roads, buildings, and public spaces

Finance: manages the municipality's money

Chapter 1 Local Government

Municipal Council Decision Making

Before a municipal council makes a decision about an issue or project, it will usually ask for advice from experts. For example, the council may ask municipal department heads for advice. Often, the council will ask a standing committee to do further research. Or, the council might create a special committee to do this job. After the committee finishes its research, it reports back to the council. A decision can now be made.

How a Local Council Might Make a Decision

1. A councillor identifies the need for improving roads to solve the problem of heavy traffic and makes a proposal to the council.

2. The council discusses the proposal and creates a committee to explore the project.

3. The committee investigates the idea for improving roads, consulting with different people and groups.
   - Municipal Department Heads
   - Engineers
   - Road Construction Experts
   - Environmentalists
   - Community Members

4. The committee creates a report for council and suggests certain actions.

5. The council discusses the report and asks questions.

6. Councillors make a decision by voting on whether or not to go ahead with the project.

Local councils make decisions about many issues that affect your daily life. From the crosswalk on a busy street to the recycling bin in a park, all services involve decisions.

Explore and Apply

1. Why would it be important for a municipal council to discuss its plans with experts and people in the community before making decisions?

2. Find an article about a project or an issue that your local council is working on. Create a flowchart showing the steps the council might take to make its decision, including the people that the council might talk to for advice.

What Do Local Governments Do?

Local governments work toward the common good when they provide services and create laws to benefit citizens in their area.

Providing Services

Local governments provide many different types of services, including the following:

- social
- transportation
- arts and culture
- safety and protection

Safety and protection services protect the lives and property of people in the community. These services include fire protection, police, and ambulance. Transportation services include building and maintaining roads, sidewalks, and transportation systems (such as buses and subways). Local governments are also responsible for keeping roads clear of snow and ice.

Catholic Connection

Our Church teaches that it is the role of government and citizens to act for the sake of the common good.

Faith in Action

In 2012, students and staff of the Sudbury Catholic District School Board in Ontario collected over 1500 pairs of shoes and boots to provide warm, dry footwear for those in need in the area.

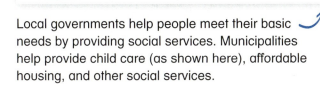

Local governments help people meet their basic needs by providing social services. Municipalities help provide child care (as shown here), affordable housing, and other social services.

Municipalities encourage arts and culture in communities. In 2010, the city of Victoria, British Columbia, hired sculptor Barbara Paterson to create this sculpture of artist Emily Carr. The statue shows Carr with her sketchpad on her lap and her pet monkey perched on her shoulder. What does the artwork you see around you suggest about your community and what it values?

Making Bylaws

Can you imagine what a hockey game would be like if there were no rules? In the same way, what would your community be like without rules? One of the roles of local governments is to make local rules, called **bylaws**. These bylaws help the community run smoothly and keep people safe.

Did You Know?

If you feed the squirrels in Mississauga, Ontario, you are breaking the law and could get fined as much as $5000! It is illegal to feed any wild animal in Mississauga, except for songbirds. Why do you think a municipality might make such a bylaw?

Most municipalities have bylaws that require homeowners to shovel their sidewalk within a certain length of time after a snowfall. How does a bylaw like this contribute to the common good?

Some Bylaws from Ontario Communities

Some Areas for Bylaws	Example of Bylaw
Safety and Security	No person shall set off fireworks within the city (except on Victoria Day or Canada Day). (Bylaw 0293-2001, Mississauga)
Transportation	No person shall operate a snowmobile within the city limits. (Bylaw 12852, Windsor)
Environmental	No sewage that has a temperature over 65 °C can be flushed into the sewer system. (Bylaw 2002-108, Township of Huron–Kinloss)
Parks, Recreation, and Culture	No person shall fly a powered model aircraft or sail a powered model boat in a city park. (Bylaw 2009-76, Kingston)
Animal Care and Control	No person shall keep more than three dogs in or around a single house. (Bylaw 65-08, Cambridge)
Property and Land Use	Owners must cut grass and weeds that are taller than 20 centimetres. (Bylaw 166-2011, Brampton)
Government	Members of Council shall at all times seek to advance the common good of the community that they serve. (Bylaw 3149, Kapuskasing)

24   Many Gifts Unit 1

Paying for Services

Most municipalities would like to provide more and better services. However, municipal governments only have a certain amount of money to spend. Each year, a municipal government creates a spending plan, called a **budget**. The municipality determines how much money it has, and then decides where this money is best spent.

Municipalities get some money from the federal and provincial or territorial governments. Municipalities also raise money themselves. For example, they collect money from the following:

- tickets and memberships at recreational facilities
- fees for parking, water use, and garbage collection
- licences, such as dog licences and business licences
- fines paid by people who break bylaws

However, most money that municipal governments collect comes from taxes. A **tax** is money that is paid to the government. Property taxes are paid to the municipality by homeowners and businesses. Property taxes are based on the size of the land that someone owns and the kind of building that is on it.

Example of How a Municipality Might Spend $100

- transportation: $21
- environment: $17
- housing: $4
- health: $3
- protection: $16
- other: $18
- recreation and culture: $12
- social services: $9

This graphic shows how one municipality spends its money. For example, for every $100 it has, it spends $16 on "protection," which includes police services. The "other" category includes service fees, regional planning, and charges related to money the municipality has borrowed. The spending decisions of a municipality depend on its size and the needs of its population.

Explore and Apply

1. What local government service do you think is most important? Why?

2. Create a bar graph showing how you would divide $100 among different municipal services if you were creating a budget for your community. You can offer any services you would like, but you must include $18 for the "other" category. Justify your choices.

Spotlight on Government Action

Catholic Connection

Pope Francis said, "I would like to ask all those who have positions of responsibility in economic, political, and social life, and all men and women of goodwill: Let us be protectors of creation, protectors of God's plan ... protectors of one another and of the environment."

Thinking about Significance

Former TV game show host Bob Barker came to Toronto to help protest keeping elephants in Canadian zoos. Some people claimed city councillors were influenced by Barker's fame, rather than listening to facts. Do you think Barker's fame affected the city's decision? Explain.

What to Do about the Elephants at the Toronto Zoo

The City of Toronto owns the Toronto Zoo. The municipal government created the Toronto Zoo Board to make decisions about running the zoo efficiently. The board is also sometimes involved in discussions about the welfare of the animals.

Decisions about animals in captivity are not always easy. Different people have different viewpoints about what is best for the animals. For example, four elephants died at the zoo between 2005 and 2009. The board had to make a decision about what to do with the remaining three elephants. Should the city spend millions of dollars to improve the zoo's elephant shelter? Or, should the zoo end the elephant program and move the elephants to a warmer climate?

In May 2011, the head of the zoo suggested closing the elephant exhibit. The zoo board decided to end the elephant program at the zoo, and it asked zoo officials to look for a new home for the three elephants. However, after six months, no action plan had been created.

Many elephant experts believe that elephants do not belong in any zoo because zoos do not allow elephants to roam freely over large areas. Some experts claim that zoos in colder climates are particularly bad because the elephants are forced to stay indoors for weeks at a time during cold weather.

Do elephants belong in cold climates? Support your response.

At a council meeting on October 25, 2011, Toronto city councillor Michelle Berardinetti made a surprise proposal to move the animals. She proposed moving them to the Performing Animal Welfare Society (PAWS) sanctuary in the United States. A **sanctuary** is an area reserved for wild animals. Most of the members of the city council agreed and voted in favour of the proposal.

Zoo officials and zookeepers were angry about the decision. They said this decision should have been left to zookeepers and veterinarians. However, city councillors said that the elephants belonged to the city of Toronto, so the council had the right and responsibility to make this decision.

Over the coming months, citizens, journalists, zookeepers, and councillors wrote articles, letters, and blogs. They argued both sides of the issue. In the end, the elephants were moved to PAWS in October 2013. Many people said that the council did not take enough time to learn about all the perspectives and all options.

The elephants travelled from the Toronto Zoo to California in large crates on a truck. The 4500-kilometre trip took more than 70 hours. Zookeepers were afraid that this long trip would put the elephants in danger.

Explore and Apply

1. If you were a city councillor, how would you have voted on this issue? On what would you have based your decision?

2. Create a graphic organizer to show the different viewpoints on keeping elephants in Canadian zoos. Use this organizer to create a survey to find out how people feel about this issue. Conduct your survey with people at school and family members.

What Are Band Councils?

Band councils are the local governments that serve communities on First Nations reserves. A **band** is a group of First Nations people who live in an area and share a common culture and ancestry. There are more than 600 First Nations bands across Canada. More than 130 of these bands are in Ontario.

Each band has an elected council that looks after community services and concerns. A band council is made up of a band chief and councillors. The number of councillors depends on the size of the community. Like municipal councillors, members of a band council meet to make decisions and serve on boards and committees.

Band councils are different from municipalities in that they do not report to the province or territory. Reserves were created by the federal government, and band councils work mainly with the federal government. However, band councils often cooperate with the provincial or territorial government and with neighbouring municipalities. There is a growing effort to create relationships between band councils and nearby municipalities. These relationships allow the communities to share the cost of providing some services.

The First Nations of the Ogemawahj Tribal Council

Tribal councils are made up of band chiefs or other representatives from several different bands. For example, the Ogemawahj Tribal Council has council members from six different Ontario First Nations. The bands work together to share information, knowledge, and leadership. The council's goal is to help each of the member bands develop the services they need.

The Six Nations of the Grand River, near Brantford, Ontario, is Canada's largest First Nation. Its band council is made up of a band chief and 12 councillors. The local government has 18 departments with more than 700 employees. This photo shows a paramedic from the Six Nations ambulance service, which is run by the Six Nations' Health Services Department.

Responsibilities of a Band Council

Band councils are responsible for the day-to-day operations of communities on reserves. They provide many of the same types of services as municipal governments, such as clean drinking water, sewer systems, and roads.

However, there are differences between the services that municipal councils and band councils provide. For example, band councils play a larger role in housing and education in their communities.

Paying for Services

How band councils pay for services is also different from municipalities. Band councils get most of their money from the federal government. This was part of the agreement that was made when First Nations peoples were moved onto reserves. At one time, the only money band councils had came from the federal government. The bands were not allowed to raise money through taxes. This created challenges. Band councils and the federal government often had different perspectives on how much money was needed and how it should be spent. Today, bands are allowed to raise money from taxes on their reserves. This helps pay for more and better services. However, many people believe that the federal government should be providing more money for services needed in First Nations communities.

↑ First Nations education is similar to education off the reserve, but many reserve schools also put more time into outdoor education and teaching traditional languages, values, and skills. This photo shows a school in the Six Nations of the Grand River.

Explore and Apply

1. In your own words, explain why the federal government and the band councils have different perspectives on how much money is needed and how it should be spent.

2. Create a graphic organizer to compare municipalities and band councils.

How Do Governments and Citizens Communicate?

Local governments are responsible for communicating their ideas and decisions to their communities. They also want to hear ideas from the people they serve.

There are different ways that governments and citizens communicate. Here are just a few ways:

1. Elections allow candidates to communicate their ideas to the public. **Candidates** are people running for government office. Community members can tell candidates what is important to them by contacting them or attending events where candidates are appearing. When citizens vote, they are also communicating which candidate's ideas they support.

2. Local council meetings are open to the public, so anyone can go to them, listen, and speak (with permission).

In 2010, Waterloo, Ontario, held a referendum to decide if the community should keep putting fluoride in its water system. Fluoride is a chemical known to prevent cavities, but some people fear that it has other harmful effects. Most citizens voted to stop adding this chemical to Waterloo's water.

People often communicate their ideas to government by taking part in peaceful protests. This photo shows a protestor in Ottawa, Ontario, on January 22, 2014. About 50 protestors gathered that day to tell city council to revise a transit plan that would increase traffic on local streets.

30 Many Gifts Unit 1

③ A local government might hold a public hearing on an important topic. A **public hearing** is a meeting open to everyone.

④ If an issue is especially important, a local government might also hold a referendum. A **referendum** is a process in which community members vote on whether the government should take a certain action.

Communication and Technology

Governments usually use media to communicate with the community. For example, they might use newspaper articles, TV commercials, radio ads, brochures, and flyers. Some municipal governments even show their council meetings on local TV stations. In recent years, changes in technology have given governments new ways to communicate with the public, including websites and social media.

Technology can also improve the voting process. It is now possible for people to vote online. Voting online helps people who have difficulty getting out to vote.

In 2003, Markham, Ontario, successfully introduced an Internet voting system.

Did You Know?
The city council in Kitchener, Ontario, was one of the first in Canada to use text messaging to discuss municipal issues and decisions with the public.

Faith in Action

Brittany Marentette, a student in the Windsor–Essex Catholic District School Board in Ontario used social media to plan a school protest when she heard rumours that her school's special education programs would be cut. As it turned out, classes were changing, but were not being cut. Nevertheless, this concerned student took action in the interest of social justice.

Explore and Apply

1. How would you bring an issue to the attention of your local government? Why would you choose that method?

2. Choose an issue in your community. Create a plan for how the municipal government could communicate its ideas about the issue. Include ways that the council could get ideas and feedback from the community.

Toolbox: Formulate Questions about an Issue

Formulating questions is an important part of any inquiry into an issue. Effective questions will lead you deeper into the issue. They will also help you find information related to different perspectives. Formulating questions helps you create a clear focus for your inquiry. Once you have a clear focus, you can look for answers to your questions.

There are three main types of questions: fact, opinion, and critical. Critical questions give you a deeper understanding. They help you develop judgments that you can defend with good reasons.

As you read the following material, think about the critical questions you could ask.

Critical Questions

Effective critical questions help you interpret facts and information and analyze perspectives and values. Effective critical questions can also help you probe deeper into an issue and analyze problems. For example, what factors should be considered when deciding whether to build an incinerator?

To Burn or Not to Burn?

Every year across Canada, millions of tonnes of garbage are brought to landfills, or garbage dumps. Many people worry that landfills can release harmful chemicals into the soil and water. However, other people say that this risk is very small in modern landfills. People on both sides of the argument wonder what happens when the landfills are full.

Some municipalities, such as the region of Peel, burn their garbage in large furnaces, called incinerators. People opposed to this approach say that these facilities create air pollution. The incinerators also create ash that has to be disposed of.

Supporters of incinerators say that very high temperatures are used to burn the garbage. This creates very little ash compared to the amount of garbage processed. They argue that the gases produced by burning garbage can be used to create energy, which is better than leaving garbage to rot away in landfills.

This is a landfill near Milton, Ontario.

> " … isn't it better to recover even a [small amount] of something from that product than sending it to a landfill site? "
>
> Monika Turner, Policy Director, Association of Municipalities of Ontario

Inquiry
Formulate Questions

> When you build an [incinerator], you are saying we will never get to zero waste, we are giving up that goal ... since we need to keep coming up with materials to feed the incinerator. So the incentive to recycle more goes down as a municipality.
>
> *Jo-Anne St. Godard, Executive Director, Recycling Council of Ontario*

Thinking about Perspective
Consider the different viewpoints, or perspectives, on burning garbage. Whose viewpoint do you most agree with? Why?

> I don't know if there is an amazing technological solution. We're not going to be able to vaporize the garbage. Hopefully, we educate people so they produce less waste—that's the best thing we can do.
>
> *Jim Harnum, Manager, Waste Management Division, Toronto*

> [By building an incinerator, we] can at least take the energy out, instead of putting [garbage] into the landfill.
>
> *Norman Lee, Head, Waste Management, region of Peel*

This aerial photo shows a garbage incinerator in Québec. What do you notice in this photo?

Explore and Apply

1. Who should be involved in deciding whether a community should burn its garbage?
2. What makes the above question an opinion question? How can you make it a critical question?
3. Formulate critical and probing questions for an interview with one of the people quoted on pages 32 and 33.

Pulling It Together

Father Mike Explains...
For all of us, contributing to the common good begins with involvement in our local community and communication with our local government.

See
What important issues do you see in your community? Who do these issues affect?

Reflect
Choose an issue in your community. How is it being dealt with? Do you agree with the way that it is being dealt with? Explain.

Act
Learn more about your chosen issue. Identify what you could start doing today to deal with this issue and to serve the common good.

How Can We Contribute to Our Community?

I didn't know how much local government affects my life. I also didn't realize how much I could affect my local government.

I looked online to find out more about the building of the Red Hill Valley Parkway. It was really interesting to read all the different viewpoints. I never would have thought about the different sides to the argument. I can see why it's important for people to speak up and share their opinions about city planning.

I'm glad community leaders listen to different points of view. I wonder if they would listen to kids. My friends and I are worried that not enough is being done about pollution in Hamilton. We're going to do more research and see if we can get the city leaders to listen to us.

Alex

Pollution is an issue for large cities like Hamilton, Ontario. When we take part in investigating and solving these issues, we contribute to the common good.

Summarizing

Create a word web to summarize what you have learned in this chapter. Use colours to highlight the most important ideas. Draw lines between words that you think are related. Explain to a partner the relationships you have identified.

Making Connections

Create a drawing of your community. Label at least three services that your local government provides. Beside each service, describe how it affects your life and your community.

The Bible says …

" Justice, and only justice, you shall pursue, so that you may live and occupy the land that … God is giving you. "

Deuteronomy 16:20 (NRSV)

Chapter Inquiry

Find out more about the issue you identified on page 34. Create an idea web to record facts as well as your thoughts about the issue. Next, develop three critical questions that could help you investigate this issue. Remember, you want to dig deeply into this issue so that you can really understand it.

Chapter 2

Provincial and Territorial Governments

Big Question

How do provincial and territorial governments work to support the common good?

Learning Goals

- describe the roles and responsibilities of provincial and territorial governments
- construct and analyze maps
- assess the effectiveness of actions taken by provincial and territorial governments

The Wabano Centre in Ottawa, Ontario, provides healthcare and support for Aboriginal people. The centre was designed by Douglas Cardinal, an architect of Métis and Niitsitapi (Blackfoot) heritage.

Hi, I'm Emma.

I live with my family in Ottawa, Ontario. We moved here from Cambridge Bay, Nunavut.

My sister has diabetes, so she needs to see special doctors. Cambridge Bay is very small. It doesn't have the kind of doctors my sister needs.

When my mom got a job in Ottawa, our family decided to move. Ottawa has more medical services than Cambridge Bay. It even has the Wabano Centre for Aboriginal Healing, where my sister goes.

I wish we could have stayed in Cambridge Bay. I wonder why all communities don't have the same access to healthcare.

Our Faith

The Bible teaches ...

If someone who has material possessions sees others in need yet does nothing to help them, how can the love of God be in that person?

1 John 3:17

What Are Provincial and Territorial Governments?

Provincial and territorial governments create laws, apply laws, and provide services for provinces and territories. A provincial or territorial government is usually called a **legislature**, or a **legislative assembly**. The Ontario legislature is sometimes called the **provincial Parliament**. A member of the Ontario government is called a **member of the provincial Parliament**, or an **MPP**.

Members of the legislature are elected from all parts of the province or territory. The province or territory is divided into areas called **ridings**. Each riding elects one member to the government. Each riding usually has about the same number of people. In this way, all parts of the province or territory are represented.

By law, provincial and territorial elections must be held at least once every five years. However, a provincial or territorial leader can call an election sooner if he or she chooses.

Legislatures meet in the capital city of the province or territory. The legislative building in Ontario is located in Toronto, in Queen's Park. People often use the term *Queen's Park* to refer to the Ontario government.

The 107 Ridings in Ontario, 2013

Why are there so many more ridings in the southern part of the province? Why are the sizes of the ridings so different?

Chapter 2 Provincial and Territorial Governments 37

The Party System

The 10 provinces and Yukon have a party system of government. This means that each candidate usually belongs to a political party. A **political party** is a team of candidates, leaders and citizens who have the same goals and values as the party. They share similar ideas about what is important. Each political party has a leader who has been selected by its members.

Each party has a platform. A **platform** describes what the party believes. For example, one party might believe that social programs and social justice are the most important issues. Another party might focus on the environment, jobs, or industry. Many voters consider a party's platform before they vote for a candidate.

A **candidate** is a person who runs for election in a riding. Candidates usually post signs around their ridings to make people aware that they are running for election.

Often, before an election, the leaders from all the parties come together to debate their positions on different issues. In this photo from April 29, 2013, John Cummins, Christy Clark, Adrian Dix, and Jane Sterk prepare for their TV debate. Many voters used this debate to help them decide who would lead the provincial legislature of British Columbia.

This photo from 2013 shows a campaign worker in London, Ontario. She worked for Peggy Sattler's campaign and was updating results for a provincial by-election. A **by-election** is a special election held between regular elections to fill a vacancy. As a result of this by-election, Peggy Sattler became an MP. MP Sattler is active on social issues, such as youth unemployment and prison safety.

38 Many Gifts Unit 1

The Government and the Opposition

After an election, the party with the most elected members forms the government. The leader of this party becomes the **premier**, or leader, of the province or territory.

Parties that have fewer elected members than the government are called **opposition parties**. The party that elected the second most members is the **Official Opposition**. Its leader is called the **Leader of the Official Opposition**. It is the responsibility of the Official Opposition to research and question the government's plans and actions. The opposition parties also suggest different ideas about what needs to be done.

In addition to elected members, the legislature needs many other people to help it run smoothly. This includes people such as the Speaker of the House, pages, and Hansard recorders. A **Hansard** is a word-for-word record of every debate held in the legislature. It is the Hansard recorder's job to create this record. Anyone can access and read the Hansard, so it is one way that governments communicate with the people they serve.

Catholic Connection
Saint John Paul II asked Catholics to take on leadership roles in society, which would allow them to "influence public life and direct it to the common good."

Did You Know?
Every year, about 140 Grades 7 and 8 students are chosen to work as pages in the Ontario legislature. Pages deliver documents and messages to assembly members.

The Speaker of the House keeps order, particularly when discussions between the government and the opposition get heated. On October 24, 2013, Kevin Murphy (left) became the new Speaker of the House for the Nova Scotia legislature. Speaker Murphy was paralyzed during a hockey game at the age of 14. After being appointed Speaker of the House, he told reporters, "It really shows that people, regardless of their level of physical disability, can do anything at all."

Cabinets and Cabinet Ministers

The premier selects members from his or her party to act as trusted advisers. This group of advisers is called the **cabinet**. Its members are called **cabinet ministers**. Each minister is usually responsible for a department of the government. For example, there is usually a Minister of Education, a Minister of Health, and a Minister of Agriculture.

The Leader of the Official Opposition selects members of the opposition to watch the actions of the government. These people are called **opposition critics**. There might be an Education Critic, a Health Critic, and an Agriculture Critic to match the ministers in the government's cabinet.

This photo shows the Ontario legislature. The legislature is open to the public. Anyone can sit in the public gallery and watch as the members discuss issues.

Consensus Government

The Northwest Territories and Nunavut use consensus government instead of a party system. A **consensus government** reaches decisions by considering the opinions of all members of the legislative assembly. Any decision made is one that all members can accept. This is the traditional form of government for many First Nations and Inuit.

As in other parts of Canada, candidates in the Northwest Territories and Nunavut are elected in ridings. However, candidates do not belong to parties. Instead, they present their own beliefs to voters. Voters then select the candidate whose ideas they support. Since there are no parties, the assembly members choose who will be premier, cabinet ministers, and Speaker of the House.

In both the party system and consensus government, action is taken when more than half of the members agree with a decision. However, consensus governments discuss issues and try to find an action that all members can accept. This often results in decisions where everyone agrees, which rarely happens in a party system.

Similar to other legislatures, the Speaker of the House for Nunavut uses a ceremonial mace, a staff that represents the role and responsibilities of the Speaker. When not in use, the Nunavut Speaker's mace sits atop carvings of men and women to reflect that both have an important and equal voice in the legislature. The mace was carved in 1999 by Inuit artist Inuk Charlie (shown here).

Members of Nunavut's legislative assembly sit in a circle.

Explore and Apply

1. Compare the consensus and party systems, including their seating arrangements.

2. Reread the Catholic Connection on page 39. What leadership roles do you (or can you) take in your community? How can you contribute to the common good through a leadership role? Create a plan for becoming more involved in your community.

Chapter 2 Provincial and Territorial Governments

How Are Laws Created and Applied?

Creating Laws

Provincial or territorial legislatures propose, debate, and pass laws. Any member of the legislature can propose an idea for a new law, which is called a **bill**. The bill is written down and given a number. The member then reads the bill out in the legislature. This is called the **first reading**.

A bill goes through three readings before it can become a law. After each reading, the legislature votes on whether the bill should move to the next reading. Bills are often sent to a committee to be studied more closely before the third reading. The committee provides information and may make small changes that help the legislature make a better decision.

If a bill passes all three readings, it is signed by a person who represents the British monarch. At this point, the bill becomes a law, called an **act**. This step is called **Royal Assent**. The reason this is done is because Canada was once a British territory, and the British queen or king is still Canada's head of state. The monarch's representatives are called **Lieutenant Governors** in the provinces and **Territorial Commissioners** in the territories.

> **Thinking about Cause and Consequence**
>
> Skin cancer cases have increased in the past few years, especially among young women aged 15 to 29. Some types of skin cancer can even cause death. Experts estimate that most skin cancer is caused by extreme exposure to UV radiation, including from tanning beds. Think about the reasons Bill 30 (see diagram below) was created and passed. What effect do you think the law will have?

How Bill 30 Became the *Skin Cancer Prevention Act (Tanning Beds), 2013*

First Reading: March 7, 2013, Ontario Health Minister Deb Matthews introduced Bill 30.

→ **Second Reading:** March 19, April 17, and April 30, 2013, Bill 30 was debated in the legislature.

→ **Review by Committee:** September 11 to September 24, 2013, a special committee studied the bill.

→ **Report to House:** September 24, 2013, the committee reported back to the legislature.

→ **Third Reading:** October 8 and 9, 2013, Bill 30 was given a third reading and the bill was passed.

→ **Royal Assent:** October 10, 2013, Lieutenant Governor of Ontario, David Onley, signed Bill 30.

This figure shows how Ontario's Bill 30 became the *Skin Cancer Prevention Act (Tanning Beds), 2013*. This law makes it illegal for people under 18 years of age to use tanning beds.

Applying Laws

Provincial and territorial governments are responsible for applying the laws that they make. They must also apply laws made by the federal government.

The responsibility of applying laws is handled by a province or territory's court system. The goal of the court system is to make sure everyone in a community is treated fairly. The court system is made up of different types of courts that deal with different types of laws. Most provinces and territories have at least three types of courts:

- A Court of Justice hears less serious crimes, including youth crimes, family cases, and driving offences. For example, when citizens want to fight parking tickets, they do so in a Court of Justice.

- A provincial Superior Court of Justice hears more serious cases, including violent crimes and serious family cases, such as divorce and child protection.

- A Court of Appeal hears appeals to decide if the right decision has been made by one of the other courts.

When Nunavut was created in 1999, a new court system was also created. It has only one level of court, called the Nunavut Court of Justice. This court hears all types of cases.

Judges work for the courts. They have expert knowledge of the law. Judges hear legal cases and then make decisions about what action needs to be taken.

Explore and Apply

1. In your opinion, should there be fewer readings or more readings before passing a law? Explain your answer.

2. Develop three questions about creating, passing, or applying laws. Gather and organize information to answer one of your questions.

What Services Do Provinces and Territories Provide?

Provincial and territorial governments provide many different types of services. Three important areas of responsibility are healthcare, education, and natural resources.

Healthcare

Canada's healthcare system is a huge network of doctors, clinics, and other healthcare facilities. Provincial and territorial governments are responsible for providing most healthcare services.

Providing quality medical care in a country the size of Canada has many challenges. One of the greatest challenges is the cost of building and maintaining hospitals. This cost includes hiring doctors, nurses, and other staff, as well as buying expensive equipment and medicines.

The provinces and territories get money for healthcare from the federal government. However, this money covers only part of the cost of healthcare. Provincial and territorial governments spend more money on healthcare each year than on any other service. These costs are growing.

Faith in Action

On April 10, 2013, students from the Toronto Catholic District School Board delivered hundreds of origami cranes to the Hospital for Sick Children. Students from around the district had made these cranes as symbols of hope and healing. The students at Our Lady of Sorrows Catholic School started this annual tradition.

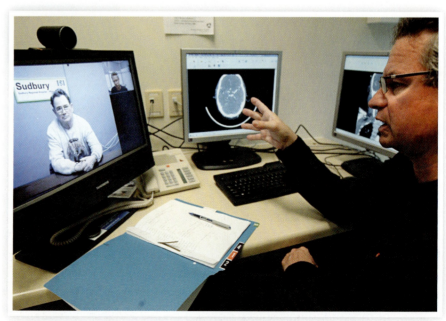

Technology is helping doctors provide care to people living in remote areas. In this photo, a doctor uses a webcam and other computer technology to diagnose and treat a patient hundreds of kilometres away.

Education

Education is the second largest area of spending for provincial and territorial governments. Provinces and territories build and take care of schools.

The goal of each Ministry of Education is to give everyone the chance to get an education. The Ministry tries to provide a learning environment that reflects the community's culture, values, and needs. For example, in Nunavut, school is taught in Inuktitut or Inuinnaqtun, which are Inuit languages. English or French is taught as another language.

Thinking about Cause and Consequence

There was an unusually large number of babies born in Canada between 1946 and 1965. How would this sudden increase in births have affected education and healthcare? Do you think that this increase in births still affects services today? Explain.

There are more than 1650 Catholic schools in Ontario, with more than 650 000 students. In this photo, students offer their support to a Grade 6 teacher at St. Matthew Catholic School. The teacher is growing a moustache for Movember, a campaign to raise money for cancer research.

The Africentric Alternative School in North York, Ontario, gives students the chance to study lessons that focus on people of African heritage.

Catholic Connection

According to Catholic teachings, both governments and individuals have a moral duty to be good stewards. Pope Benedict XVI reminded us that the environment is God's gift to everyone. In our use of it, we have a responsibility toward the poor, future generations, and humanity as a whole.

Managing Natural Resources

The federal government controls the sale of land and the use of natural resources in Nunavut and the Northwest Territories. However, in the provinces and Yukon, the provincial and territorial governments control how natural resources are developed. This means that they make decisions about a number of issues. For example, they decide where mines can be built, which forests can be harvested, and how farms have to operate.

In Ontario, different ministries look after the environment and natural resources.

- The Ministry of Agriculture and Food oversees farms and food safety.
- The Ministry of the Environment looks into environmental issues, such as pollution, endangered species, and sustainable sources of energy.
- The Ministry of Natural Resources manages resources throughout Ontario, including forests, minerals, and water.
- The Ministry of Northern Development and Mines manages economic development in northern Ontario, especially for the mining industry.

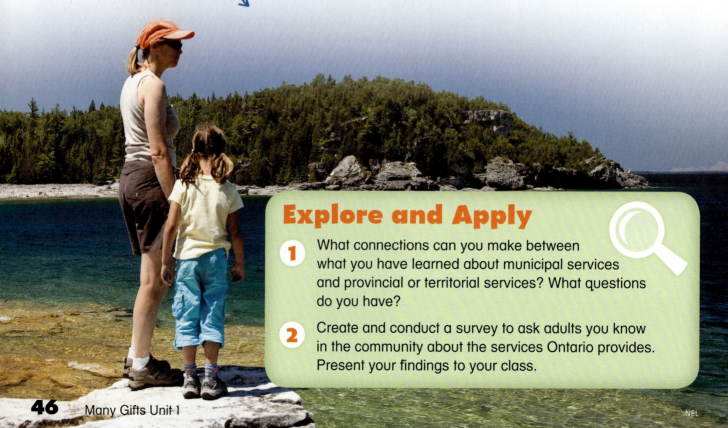

This photo shows part of the Bruce Trail that runs through the Niagara Escarpment. The Niagara Escarpment is a protected area in Ontario. The Ontario Ministry of Natural Resources is responsible for provincial parks, conservation areas, and protected areas.

Explore and Apply

1. What connections can you make between what you have learned about municipal services and provincial or territorial services? What questions do you have?

2. Create and conduct a survey to ask adults you know in the community about the services Ontario provides. Present your findings to your class.

How Do Provinces and Territories Pay for Services?

Provincial and territorial governments get money from taxes and from the federal government. They have to create a budget. A government calculates how much money it can raise through taxes so that it knows how much it can spend. It then decides which services it can afford to provide.

Five Largest Areas of Expense in the Ontario Budget for 2013—2014

health and long-term care — $38
education — $19
children's and social services — $11
training, colleges, and universities — $6
justice — $3

This diagram shows how the Ontario government assigns money to five of its departments. For example, for every $100 the government spends, it spends $38 on health and long-term care.

Governments do not have unlimited money to pay for services. Often, this leads to difficult decisions. Should they stop providing certain services? Should they make people pay for some services? Should they borrow money to pay for services? Should they raise taxes to pay for services?

These are difficult questions that often become very important during elections. Different political parties usually have very different answers. Their answers affect how people vote.

Did You Know?

You pay taxes. Every time you buy something, part of the money you pay goes to the government as a tax. This is called a sales tax. If you buy a $10 game in Ontario, you pay an extra $1.30 in tax.

Faith in Action

Sometimes taxes are not enough and schools have to find other ways to get resources. For example, teacher Elissa Zuliana from St. Raphael Catholic School in Sudbury, Ontario, created a video with her special needs students. They entered the video in a 2014 contest to win money to purchase technology resources for their classroom. They won $5000.

Explore and Apply

1. Why do you think more money is spent on healthcare and education than other services?

2. You want to become premier of Ontario. Write a short speech. Describe how you would improve services and explain how you would pay for those improved services.

Spotlight on Ontario's *Far North Act*

On October 25, 2010, the Ontario government passed Bill 191, which became the *Far North Act*. The act was passed to protect boreal forest in northern Ontario. Bill 191 restricts the number of trees that can be cut down. It also restricts other developments. Trees clean pollutants from the air. Scientists believe that saving large forested areas helps fight climate change.

There are 49 First Nations communities in the area covered by the *Far North Act*. They are represented by the Nishnawbe Aski Nation. Leaders of this nation say that this act takes away future opportunities for First Nations communities to develop resources on their lands. Leaders say that they support all efforts to protect the environment, but the needs of their people must be considered. They believe that the Ontario government has forced this act through without listening to the concerns of First Nations peoples.

The wolverine is one of the many species that is protected as a result of the *Far North Act*. The wolverine is a member of the weasel family. It is sometimes mistaken for a small bear.

Compare this map to the map on page 37. What do you notice?

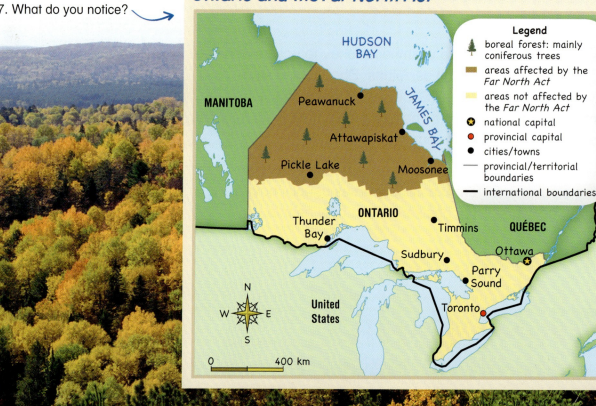

48   Many Gifts Unit 1

> 66 Our legislation puts Ontario among world leaders in forest protection, providing one of the largest land protection commitments in North America to fight climate change. 99

Michael Gravelle, former Minister of Natural Resources, Ontario

> 66 First Nations must have a say in how and when our land will be developed. Bill 191 takes away that right for our remote communities in the far north. 99

Stan Beardy, former Grand Chief, Nishnawbe Aski Nation

The *Far North Act* affects people, businesses, and economic development throughout northern Ontario. This photo shows a motel on the Moose River, near Moosonee, Ontario. How do you think the owner of this motel reacted to the *Far North Act*?

> 66 Imagine if you tried to ... declare half of southern Ontario off limits—no agriculture, no housing, no industry. There would be a revolt here. The *Far North Act* is simply bad public policy. 99

Norm Miller, MPP, Parry Sound–Muskoka

> 66 Overall, we agree with the act and we see that there is value.... The *Far North Act* affects us [all], and we want to ensure it is carried out in a responsible ... manner that respects all northern groups—be they businesses, municipalities, or First Nations. 99

Julie Denomme, vice chair, Greater Sudbury Chamber of Commerce

Explore and Apply

1. Discuss the different perspectives on the *Far North Act*. What questions do these perspectives raise?

2. If a reporter asked you what you thought about the *Far North Act*, what would you say? Use the information and quotations on this page as the basis for your own statement supporting or opposing the *Far North Act*.

Chapter 2 Provincial and Territorial Governments

Toolbox: Construct and Analyze Maps

Map Features

Your map may need all or most of the following features:

- a title
- a compass rose
- labels
- symbols
- a scale
- a legend

When constructing a map, you should decide the following:

1. What is the purpose of your map? What are you trying to communicate? Is a map the best way to present this information visually? You can help your reader understand your purpose by using a title that reflects what your map is meant to communicate.

2. What geographic area are you discussing? This area should be the focus of your map.

3. What information do you need to provide to get your message across? What is the best way to present this information: using colours, symbols, or both? What labels will you need? Include a legend to make it clear what the colours and symbols mean.

Emma created this map based on information she found on government websites.

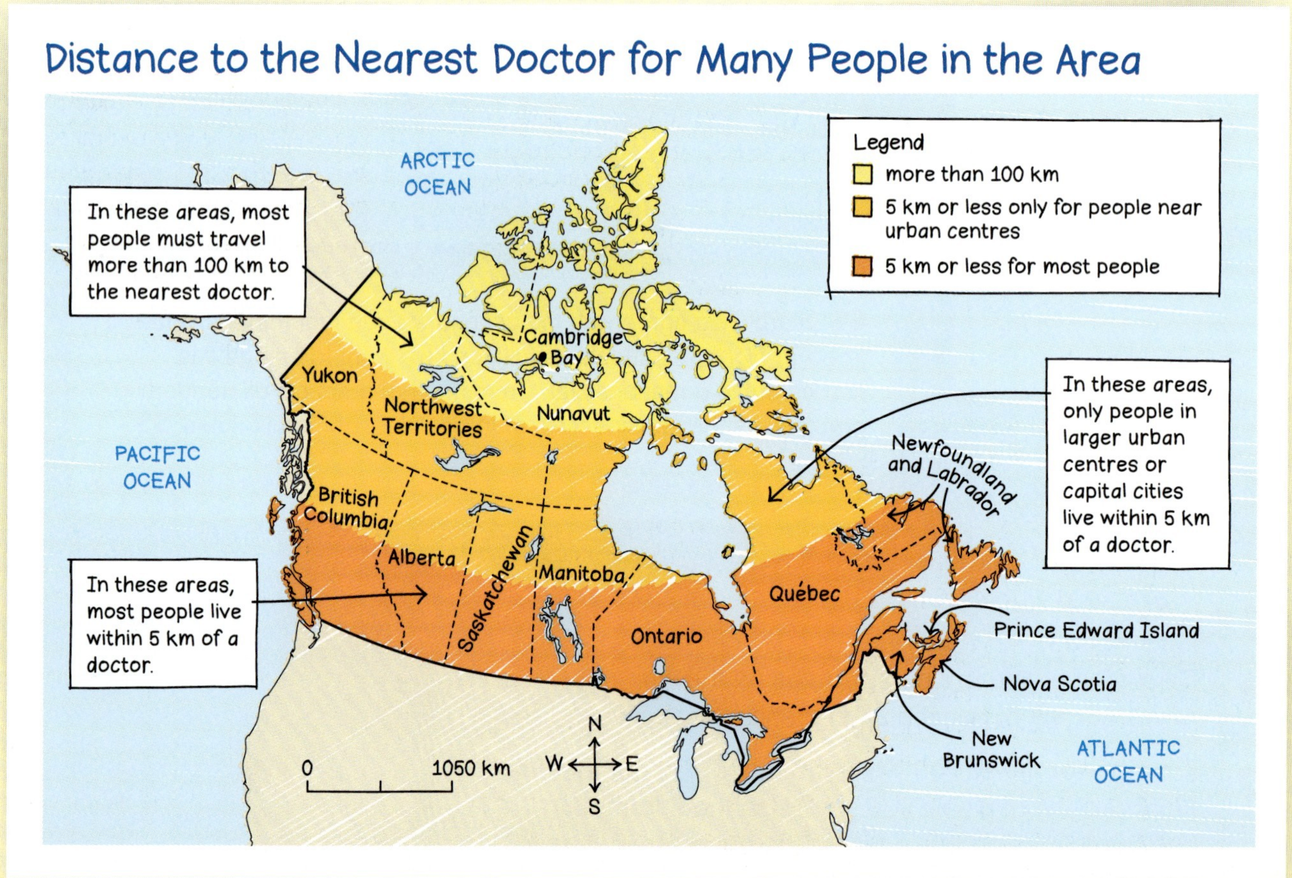

Distance to the Nearest Doctor for Many People in the Area

Legend
- more than 100 km
- 5 km or less only for people near urban centres
- 5 km or less for most people

In these areas, most people must travel more than 100 km to the nearest doctor.

In these areas, most people live within 5 km of a doctor.

In these areas, only people in larger urban centres or capital cities live within 5 km of a doctor.

Labels: Arctic Ocean, Pacific Ocean, Atlantic Ocean, Yukon, Northwest Territories, Nunavut, Cambridge Bay, British Columbia, Alberta, Saskatchewan, Manitoba, Ontario, Québec, Newfoundland and Labrador, Prince Edward Island, Nova Scotia, New Brunswick

Scale: 0 – 1050 km

Many Gifts Unit 1

Inquiry
Interpret and Analyze

Emma asked Felix, her classmate, for feedback. Felix followed these steps to analyze the map:

1. Read the title to understand the map's purpose. Examine the map, especially the legend, to see how the information relates to the map's title.

2. Monitor your comprehension of the map. What parts of the map don't make sense to you? What questions do you have about the map?

3. Make connections to other maps or information. What do you know that will help you understand the map?

Felix remembered seeing a map that showed Canada's population. He remembered that more people live in southern Canada than northern Canada. By thinking about both maps, he drew the conclusion that there were more doctors in southern Canada because there were more people there.

Number of Family Doctors, by Population, 2011

Province/Territory	Number of Family Doctors	Approximate Population	Approximate Population per Doctor
Ontario	17 135	12 852 000	750
Nunavut	14	32 000	2286

Sometimes, after creating and analyzing a map, you may have more questions or want to investigate further. For example, Emma wanted to find out more about the relationship between population and number of doctors. She discovered the information in this chart. She wondered how that affected healthcare in places that are farther north.

Explore and Apply

1. Analyze the map on page 50. What feedback do you think Felix gave Emma? Is there any other information you would like added to the map? Explain.

2. Like Emma, your family is on the move. Find three maps of Canada that help to show why a particular part of Canada would be your first choice. Consider both government services and geographic features. Use the three maps to explain your choice. Create a new map that shows all of the benefits of living in your chosen province, region, or city.

Pulling It Together

Father Mike Explains...

Pope Francis, looking at the suffering of so many in our world, asked, "Have we forgotten that we are brothers and sisters?"

See

Are there people in your community that do not have access to the services they need? Explain.

Reflect

We care for one another by helping out personally (we call this charity). We also do so by making sure our government provides the services people need (we call this justice). How do you care for others?

Act

Create a web page to promote the need to provide services that care for others. Show why both government and citizens need to be involved.

How Can We Contribute to the Common Good?

I think it's really important that our government listens to what different people think. Our leaders need to know what is important to us and what we need.

I think the Ontario provincial government proved it was listening when it helped build the Wabano Centre for Aboriginal Healing in Ottawa. It really helps my sister and many other people in our community.

I hope the provincial government keeps trying to do more to help all communities get good healthcare. One day, I would like to become a doctor and work back in Cambridge Bay.

Emma

Children and adults in Ontario protest to get the government to stop cutting hospital budgets.

Many Gifts Unit 1

Summarizing

Create a dialogue between an official from a provincial or territorial government and an official from a local government. In your dialogue, show some differences and similarities between the two levels of government. You may want to focus your dialogue on the responsibilities of each level of government, the services they provide, or an issue connected with each level.

Making Connections

Make connections between what you have learned about provincial government and news stories that you have read, heard, or seen. How does the information in this chapter help you to understand those stories?

The Bible teaches …

If someone who has material possessions sees others in need yet does nothing to help them, how can the love of God be in that person?

1 John 3:17

Chapter inquiry

Reflect on the Big Question from the beginning of this chapter: How do provincial and territorial governments work to support the common good? Analyze the maps and other information in this chapter to help you think about this question.

Choose one specific issue, such as healthcare. Gather other information to help you assess how effectively the government addresses this issue. Share your findings with a partner.

Chapter 3

Federal Government

Big Question

How does the federal government promote the common good?

Learning Goals

- describe the roles and responsibilities of the federal government
- gather and organize information
- assess the effectiveness of actions taken by the federal government

Hi, I'm Angelica.

I live with my family in London, Ontario. We moved here from the Philippines. At first I missed home. Once we settled in and met some people, things were much easier.

My parents volunteer with Canada's Host Program. The Canadian government created this program to help immigrants settle into the community. My mom and dad show families where things are and how to get around. They also help them meet new friends. Sometimes I go with my parents to talk to other kids about Canada.

I've learned a bit about Canada and how I can help. I wonder what else citizens and the Canadian government can do to help newcomers.

Our federal government is based in Ottawa, Ontario. Parliament Hill, in Ottawa, is the most recognized symbol of the federal government. On July 1st, citizens gather here to celebrate Canada's birthday.

Our Faith

The Bible says ...

"For I was hungry and you gave me food, I was thirsty and you gave me something to drink, I was a stranger and you welcomed me...."

Matthew 25:35–37 (NRSV)

What Is Federal Government?

Canada is a federation of provinces and territories. A **federation** is a group made up of smaller groups that agree to work together. Each province or territory has its own government, but the federal government makes decisions that affect all of the federation's members.

The document that describes the agreement between the provinces, territories, and federal government is called the Canadian Constitution. The **Canadian Constitution** describes the relationship between the different levels of government. It also describes their roles and responsibilities. According to the Canadian Constitution, some areas of responsibility are shared by different levels of government. For example, the federal and provincial or territorial governments share responsibility for agriculture.

This photo shows a migrant farm worker harvesting cranberries in British Columbia. **Migrant workers** are workers who travel around from place to place looking for seasonal work, such as planting or harvesting. Unlike immigrants, migrant workers are allowed into the country for only a short period of time. Migrant workers are a federal responsibility.

Explore and Apply

1. What ideas do you have about why migrant workers are a federal responsibility?

2. Begin a KWL chart for Canada's federal government. Add to the chart as you work through the chapter.

How Is Canada's Federal Government Structured?

Canada's federal government has three branches that work together to govern Canada, as shown in the figure below.

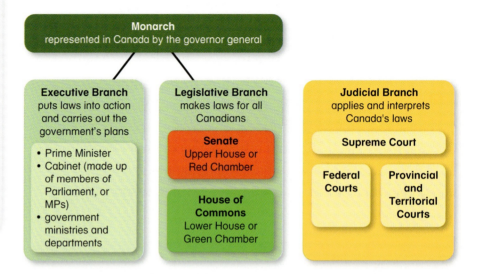

Catholic Connection

Major General Georges Vanier was Canada's governor general from 1959 to 1967. He and his wife, Pauline Vanier, started the Vanier Institute of the Family. This organization promotes the well-being of families in Canada. In 1992, the Catholic Church started the process to make them saints.

The Monarch

The British monarch (king or queen) is Canada's Head of State. Since the monarch does not live in Canada, a representative for the monarch is appointed. This representative is called the **governor general** and is part of the federal government.

This photo shows former Governor General Michaëlle Jean and her daughter with the British monarch, Queen Elizabeth II. The British monarch once had the power to make decisions for Canada, including if Canada went to war. Today, decisions such as these are made by the prime minister and his or her cabinet.

56 Many Gifts Unit 1

The Executive Branch

The executive branch is made up of the governor general, the prime minister, the cabinet, and all the departments. Together, they deliver federal services. The people who work for government departments are called **public servants**. There are more than 275 000 public servants in Canada.

The prime minister is the leader of Canada's government. He or she leads the party that has the most elected members. Elected members of the federal government are called **members of Parliament**, or MPs. The **cabinet** is a group of MPs, or cabinet ministers, selected by the prime minister to provide advice and share the responsibility of leadership.

The word *government* can be used to describe all the people and institutions that govern Canada. This word can also be used to describe just the ruling party: the prime minister and his or her cabinet.

The executive branch of Canada's federal government executes, or acts on, the laws and policies passed by the legislative branch.

Public servants include scientists, translators, inspectors, researchers, advisers, park rangers, and customs officers. Why do you think scientists, like the one in this photo, might be hired by the federal government?

The Legislative Branch

The legislative branch of the federal government is made up of the governor general, the Senate, and the House of Commons. We often refer to the legislative branch as **Parliament**. The main job of Parliament is to propose and pass bills. If passed, or approved, these bills become laws.

The Senate

The Senate is made up of 105 members, called **senators**. The prime minister chooses senators from different regions of Canada. The senators advise the House of Commons on decisions. Laws in Canada have to be passed by both the Senate and the House of Commons.

The House of Commons

The House of Commons is made up of the prime minister and all other members of Parliament. Members of the governing party, including the prime minister, sit on one side of the House. All other MPs sit on the other side. They are the opposition parties. The **Official Opposition** is the party with the second-most MPs. The leader of this party is called the **Leader of the Official Opposition**.

All MPs meet in the House of Commons to hear reports and to discuss and vote on bills. There is also a time, called Question Period, when opposition MPs ask questions of the governing party.

> **Did You Know?**
> The word *parliament* comes from the French word *parler*, which means "to speak." It is the responsibility of Parliament to speak for all Canadians.

The Senate house, or chamber, is sometimes referred to as the Upper House or the Red Chamber.

The House of Commons is sometimes referred to as the Lower House or the Green Chamber.

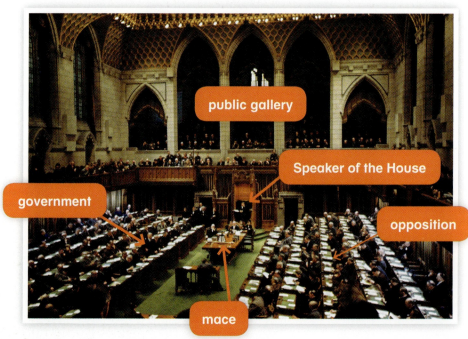

The Judicial Branch

The judicial branch of the federal government is Canada's court system. It includes provincial courts, the Federal Court of Canada, and the Supreme Court of Canada.

The Federal Court of Canada deals with cases that involve the federal government or areas controlled by the federal government. For example, in 2012, First Nations groups claimed that the federal government discriminated against First Nations children by not providing certain services for children on reserves.

The Supreme Court of Canada is Canada's highest court. It hears cases that are important to the whole country. It also gives advice to the provincial and federal governments to ensure that the laws and policies they make do not go against the Constitution. As well, the Supreme Court often decides whether a lower court has made the right decision. The Supreme Court's decisions cannot be overruled by politicians or other courts.

There are nine judges, or justices, on the Supreme Court. The Chief Justice, who leads the Supreme Court, is the Right Honourable Beverley McLachlin (front row, centre). She was appointed as Canada's Chief Justice in 2000 and is the first woman to hold this position.

This southern mountain woodland caribou is one of many threatened species in Canada. In 2014, one federal court case was about how the Ministry of the Environment was not acting quickly enough to save the caribou and other species.

Explore and Apply

1. What questions do you still have about the branches of the federal government?

2. Create a diagram to show your understanding of how the federal government is structured.

Who Are Members of the Federal Government?

Members of Parliament are elected from across the country so that every part of the country is represented in the federal government. Federal elections must be held at least once every five years.

The number of representatives that each province or territory has in the federal government generally depends on population. This idea is called **representation by population**. Provinces and territories with larger populations have more representatives. In the 2011 federal election, there were 308 MPs elected from across Canada. However, the federal government decided in 2011 that some provinces with growing populations should have more MPs for the 2015 election.

Did You Know?

In the past, some Canadians were denied their right to vote in federal elections. Here are the years in which some Canadians were first allowed to vote in federal elections:

- 1918: some women
- 1948 and 1949: Canadians of Asian origin
- 1960: all Inuit and First Nations peoples
- 2000: Canadians who are homeless
- 2002: Canadians in prisons

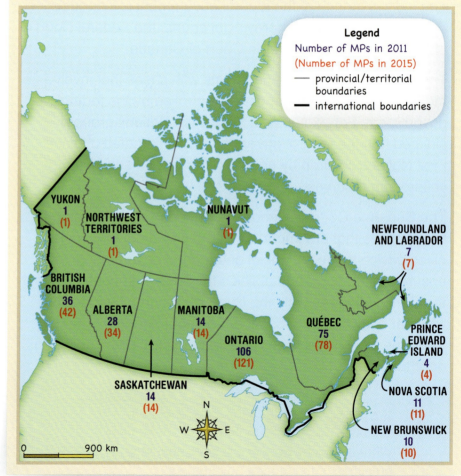

MPs from Across Canada, 2011/2015

60   Many Gifts Unit 1

Federal Political Parties

Almost all candidates in a federal election belong to a political party. In 2013, there were 17 official federal political parties. However, most federal parties do not get enough votes to have a member elected. In 2011, only five parties had one or more members elected to the House of Commons.

Results of the 2011 Federal Election

Party	Number of MPs
Conservative Party	166
New Democratic Party	103
Liberal Party of Canada	34
Bloc Québécois	4
Green Party of Canada	1

This chart shows the five political parties that had one or more members elected to the House of Commons in 2011. Identify the party that formed the government and the party that formed the Official Opposition.

Canadians have the right to form, join, and support a federal political party that reflects their values and interests. This poster is for the *parti rhinocéros* (Rhinoceros Party). This political party's slogan is "We promise to keep none of our promises."

Explore and Apply

1. In your opinion, is it fair for provinces and territories with larger populations to have more MPs? Why, or why not?

2. Propose a new federal political party to help those in need. How will your party reflect your Catholic faith? Name your new party and create a logo for it.

Faith in Action

At St. Agnes Catholic Elementary School in Stoney Creek, Ontario, teachers, staff, and students go out of their way to make newcomers feel at home. As one student says, "When a class has new students, we all make them feel welcome. If someone gives new students any trouble, we will stand up for them. We try to make them feel that they will always be safe and have friends at St. Agnes."

Did You Know?

Early in Canada's history, the Northwest Mounted Police delivered mail in the west. This police force later became the Royal Canadian Mounted Police, or RCMP.

What Services Does the Federal Government Provide?

The federal government is responsible for areas important to all Canadians. This includes Aboriginal affairs, public safety, foreign trade, justice, immigration, citizenship, natural resources, fisheries and oceans, and money and banking. The photos on this page show examples of some of these services.

The federal government oversees all types of transportation between provinces and territories and between Canada and other countries. This is an aerial photo of Toronto Pearson International Airport. This airport handles more than 30 million passengers a year.

The federal government ensures that mail is delivered. In 2013, Canada Post reviewed the service it provides. Because of budget concerns, it has eliminated door-to-door mail delivery in many communities. This affects everyone, but is of particular concern to seniors or those with disabilities.

The federal government prints Canada's currency, or money.

The federal government oversees the Canadian military, which protects Canada and helps in times of disaster.

The federal government is responsible for soldiers after they leave Canada's Armed Forces. This is called Veterans Affairs. This photo shows Master Corporal Paul Franklin with physical therapist Bev Agur. He is currently leading a protest about how Canada treats its veterans.

The federal government provides many services for new immigrants. For example, they provide help with learning English and French, finding a job or a place to live, and filling out forms. They also provide newcomers with information about living in Canada and about community services.

The federal government watches over trade between provinces and territories as well as trade with other countries. Container ships like this one carry goods back and forth to Canada. There are many regulations about what can be shipped into and out of Canada.

Explore and Apply

1. Should the federal government be responsible for the services shown on pages 62 and 63, or could another level of government provide them? Explain your answer.

2. Investigate one of the services shown on pages 62 and 63 or another federal service of your choice. Write a critical question to guide your inquiry.

Spotlight on Arctic Sovereignty

What Is Arctic Sovereignty?

Sovereignty means having legal control over an area. If a country holds sovereignty over a piece of land or water, the government has the right to move freely through the area and take resources from it. Canada has sovereignty over its land and waters. The federal government is responsible for defending Canada's rights to these areas. They are also responsible for protecting the country's borders.

A huge part of Canada's territory is in the Arctic, including large parts of the Arctic Ocean. However, Canada is not the only country with coastline on the Arctic Ocean and a claim to this region.

Scientists believe that there are huge deposits of oil in the Arctic. There are also resources, such as iron ore and diamonds. This means that more countries are becoming interested in developing industry in this region.

To protect Canada's claim to the Arctic, the federal government created the settlements of Grise Fiord and Resolute in the 1950s. The government forced several Inuit families to move to those areas. The families struggled to start new lives, with little government support. In 2010, the government apologized for this action. Artist Looty Pijamini created this sculpture in Grise Fiord to honour the families.

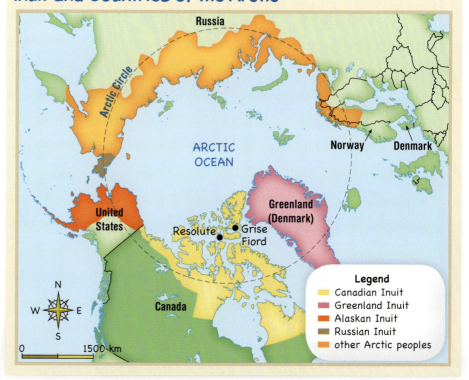

Inuit and Countries of the Arctic

This map shows the Arctic Ocean, viewed from above the North Pole. The federal government believes that the presence of Canadian Inuit in this region supports Canada's claim. In 1984, the United Nations granted certain areas of the Arctic sea floor to Canada, the United States, Russia, Norway, and Denmark.

Legend
- Canadian Inuit
- Greenland Inuit
- Alaskan Inuit
- Russian Inuit
- other Arctic peoples

The Canadian government is taking action to defend its claims to parts of the Arctic. This sometimes means putting military ships and people in the area.

Volunteer soldiers, called Canadian Rangers, help patrol Canada's North. Many Canadian Rangers are Inuit who live in the region.

The Canadian Armed Forces run drills in different parts of the Arctic, such as practising search-and-rescue missions.

The Canadian government sends scientists into the Arctic area to study climate and wildlife, as well as to look for historical artifacts.

Canadian Coast Guard icebreakers, such as this one, patrol Arctic waters.

Explore and Apply

1. Do you think the types of activities described above strengthen Canada's claim to sovereignty? Support your answer.

2. What else could Canada do to strengthen Arctic sovereignty? Construct a map showing your ideas.

Thinking about Perspective

Consider different perspectives on sovereignty in the North. Who else do you think needs to be considered in a discussion of the right to Arctic land and water?

Who Represents Aboriginal Peoples?

According to the Canadian Constitution, the federal government is responsible for working with Aboriginal peoples to provide services and honour agreements. However, Aboriginal peoples had their own forms of government long before Europeans came to what is now Canada. These governments had jurisdiction over their lands and communities. Aboriginal peoples lost most of the power they once had to make decisions for their communities.

Today, Aboriginal peoples are fighting to have their right to govern themselves recognized by the Canadian government. There are national First Nations, Inuit, and Métis organizations involved in this effort. These organizations ensure that Aboriginal concerns are heard. As well, they try to get the Canadian government to honour agreements that were made with their peoples.

Assembly of First Nations

The Assembly of First Nations speaks for First Nations across Canada. It meets with the Canadian government to discuss issues such as territorial rights, education, healthcare, and language.

Background History

After Canada became a country in 1867, Aboriginal peoples were forced onto reserves and had to use European forms of government. The federal government controlled many of their decisions. These included decisions about services such as healthcare and education.

This photo shows federal Health Minister Leona Aglukkaq (front left) and Assembly of First Nations (AFN) Chief Shawn Atleo (front right) meeting in 2011. In that year, First Nations in British Columbia made an agreement with the Canadian government that allowed them to make decisions about healthcare services. The AFN helped with this agreement.

Inuit Tapiriit Kanatami

The Inuit Tapiriit Kanatami (ITK) represents Inuit living across Northern Canada. There are four Inuit regions in Canada. After years of discussion, the federal government now recognizes that Nunavut and Nunatsiavut have their own governments. The ITK played a role in helping to make this happen. It continues to work to get the federal government to recognize the right to self-government for the other two regions.

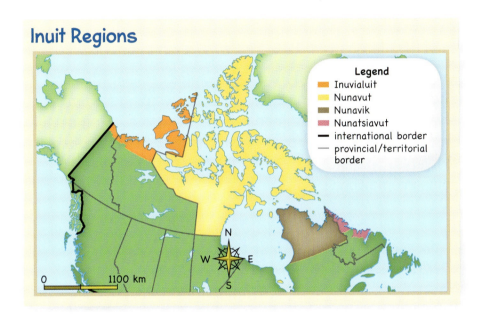

Inuit Regions

Métis National Council

Métis are people of both First Nations and European ancestry. Their history goes back hundreds of years to the time when Europeans first arrived in Canada. However, it was not until the Canadian Constitution was changed in 1982 that the Canadian government recognized the Métis as a unique people, with special rights. Today, the Métis National Council (MNC) represents many Métis across Canada. Its goals include promoting Métis culture and self-government.

Explore and Apply

1. Why is it important for First Nations, Inuit, and Métis to have organizations that represent them?

2. Find a recent news article about how Aboriginal peoples and the federal government are trying to resolve an issue. Create a graphic organizer to show all sides of the issue.

Toolbox: Gather and Organize Information

Gathering Information

1. Consider where to find the answer to your inquiry question (for example, library, Internet, pamphlets, interviews).

2. List key words and phrases that might help you find information.

3. Investigate using a variety of resources (for example, Internet, videos, books, magazines, newspapers).

Angelica wondered: Where do immigrants settle in Canada? She searched the Internet, using the key words *government* and *immigration*. She learned that the Canadian government creates Welcome Centres to help immigrants, or permanent residents. On the Statistics Canada website, she gathered some information.

Catholic Connection

Catholic social teaching urges us as a nation to be especially caring and generous in welcoming refugees to our country. **Refugees** are people who are forced to move from their homes because of war or mistreatment.

Thinking about Patterns and Trends

The Canadian government has established Welcome Centres in communities across the country to provide support for immigrants. Based on the information on this page, where should the government build these Welcome Centres? What patterns would the government need to identify to help with this decision?

Where Permanent Residents Settled

Province/Territory	2010	2012
Ontario	118 114	99 154
Québec	53 982	55 062
British Columbia	44 183	36 241
Alberta	32 642	36 092
Manitoba	15 809	13 312
Saskatchewan	7 615	11 177
Prince Edward Island	2 581	2 211
Nova Scotia	2 408	1 088
New Brunswick	2 125	2 341
Newfoundland and Labrador	714	731
Yukon	350	273
Northwest Territories	137	166
Nunavut	19	20

After you gather information, review what you have found. Reflect on your question. Ask yourself if you have enough information and whether you have any new questions.

Inquiry
Gather and Organize Information

Organizing Information

1. Look for connections between pieces of information.

2. Sort your information into different categories. Ask yourself: Are there other ways to sort the information? Should I use a graphic organizer? If so, what type of graphic organizer should I use?

3. Organizing your information can help you with your next step, interpreting and analyzing. Once your information is organized, identify any relationships and patterns.

Angelica then wondered where immigrants in London, Ontario, came from. She used this map to organize the information she found.

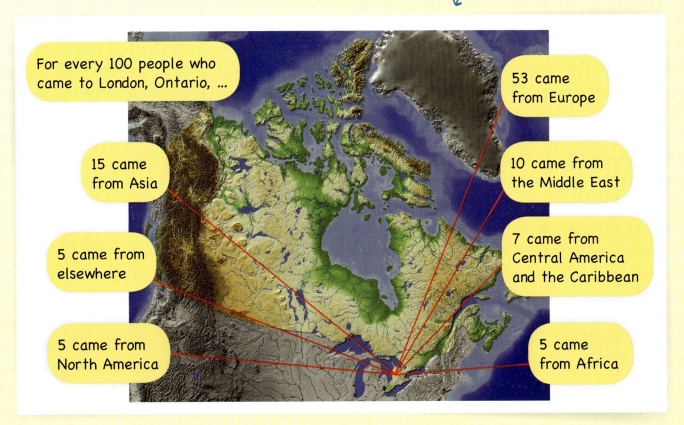

For every 100 people who came to London, Ontario, …
- 53 came from Europe
- 10 came from the Middle East
- 7 came from Central America and the Caribbean
- 5 came from Africa
- 5 came from North America
- 5 came from elsewhere
- 15 came from Asia

Explore and Apply

1. How else could Angelica organize this information to help answer her second inquiry question?

2. Find immigration data for your community for the past five years. Organize that data in a useful way.

Chapter 3 Federal Government

Pulling It Together

Father Mike Explains...

Every individual in a group benefits from the good that the group creates. This is the common good. Individual Canadians benefit from having a caring federal government that provides such things as an immigration program, defence against invaders, and a healthcare system.

See

Make connections to this chapter and to the services that the federal government provides to care for its citizens.

Reflect

Reflect on how well the federal government cares for its citizens. Identify areas that you think could be improved.

Act

Write a letter or email to your member of Parliament, expressing any concerns that you have about how the federal government is caring for its citizens.

How Does the Federal Government Work for the Common Good?

I didn't realize how huge a job it is to govern a country, particularly one as big as Canada! The federal government has to consider the needs of so many people.

I'm glad our government works to hear different perspectives. I think it's important that there are organizations to represent peoples' interests, such as the Assembly of First Nations. All Canadians should be able to have their voices heard.

I'm also proud to live in a country that cares for people who are in need. Programs like the immigrant Host Program show how important it is to help one another. When I grow up, I'm going to continue to be part of the Host Program. Maybe I'll even get a job helping to run it!

Angelica

The young girl in this photo shares her pride in becoming a new Canadian.

Summarizing

You have now studied the local, provincial and territorial, and federal levels of government. Create a graphic organizer that summarizes what you know about each level.

Making Connections

Use the graphic organizer that you created in the Summarizing activity to help you make connections between the different levels of government. What do you notice? What strikes you as important?

The Bible says …

 For I was hungry and you gave me food, I was thirsty and you gave me something to drink, I was a stranger and you welcomed me….

Matthew 25:35–37 (NRSV)

Chapter Inquiry

Develop an inquiry question for an investigation into a federal issue, such as postal service or Veterans Affairs. Gather at least five news articles connected to your issue.

With a partner who chose the same issue, review all of your articles. Organize all of the articles that you have both found. What criteria will you use to help you organize the articles? How can organizing the articles help you to answer your inquiry question?

What should the federal government do to resolve this issue? How might Canadian citizens help? Together, list some ideas for dealing with the issue.

Chapter 4

Working Together

Big Question

How do governments work together to support the common good?

Learning Goals

- describe the shared responsibilities and key actions of various levels of government
- interpret and analyze information about an issue
- assess the effectiveness of actions taken by various levels of government to address an issue

All three levels of government work together to help people find jobs. Job expos, such as the one shown here, bring together potential employees and employers.

Hi, I'm Colette.

I live in Windsor, Ontario, with my family. We love living here, but we may have to move. Mom lost her job last year when the auto factory closed.

Mom is taking classes at a local college. These classes will train her for a new job, but that job may not be in Windsor.

I wonder how our government helps people looking for work. Jobs are a really big issue in Windsor right now, but maybe not in all Ontario communities. How can Windsor work with the province and with the federal government to help people who have lost their jobs?

Our Faith

Our Church says ...

We are social beings and we need one another. The goal of social institutions, including governments, should be the protection and advancement of all people.

Why Do Governments Work Together?

Municipal governments, provincial and territorial governments, and the federal government all have their own responsibilities. However, the different levels of government often work together to make sure laws and services are similar across the country. For example, school buses must be painted the same colour in all parts of Canada: school bus yellow.

Different levels of government also work together when a service, project, or issue is too large or expensive for one level alone. For example, different levels of government are needed to create effective transportation systems.

Different levels of government are needed to organize and host large events, such as the 2010 Winter Olympics and Paralympics in Vancouver. The city of Vancouver, the government of British Columbia, and the Canadian government all shared the cost and responsibility of hosting this event.

How do you think the different levels of government might have been involved in the Paralympics and Olympics in Vancouver? Use your knowledge of all three levels to answer.

Catholic Connection

The Archbishop of Vancouver suggested that the 2010 Olympics was a building block of peace and friendship between peoples and nations.

Providing Transportation

Different levels of government work together to provide Canada's transportation systems. This includes building and maintaining sidewalks, roads, bridges, seaports, and airports. A municipal government provides local services. Other levels of government may help pay for those services. As well, many laws apply to transportation. For example, we have speed limits as well as rules about what passenger planes can carry. These laws are developed and enforced by different levels of government.

Thinking about Interrelationships

In 2012, there were more than 300 000 jobs in Canada related to mining. The industry was worth over $60 billion to the Canadian economy. How do you think the success of this industry relates to having a good transportation system?

The federal government is responsible for transportation services across Canada. For example, the federal government is responsible for regulating airports, ports, and railways.

According to the Canadian Constitution, provinces and territories are responsible for highways. The Ontario government builds more than 3000 kilometres of ice roads every year to connect 31 First Nations communities to major roads or railways.

74 Many Gifts Unit 1

Keeping Canadians Safe and Secure

Many different law enforcement agencies work to keep Canadians safe and secure. Each agency works within a particular **jurisdiction**, or area. For example, a local police force has jurisdiction only within that community. The Ontario Ministry of Environment enforces only environmental laws in Ontario. The Royal Canadian Mounted Police (RCMP) has jurisdiction across Canada.

The different law enforcement agencies sometimes share information or even work together. For example, Environment Canada deals with the crime of smuggling exotic animals into Canada. However, to investigate crimes, this agency may work with the Canada Border Services Agency.

Did You Know?
Both the Canadian Pacific Railway and Canadian National Railway have their own police forces. The officers of these forces can make arrests on railway property or within 500 metres of it.

There are law enforcement agencies that work in special areas, such as protecting forests and wildlife, inspecting restaurants, and checking mail. This photo shows an officer inspecting mail to make sure it does not contain dangerous or illegal items.

Explore and Apply

1. Why would the federal government, rather than another level of government, be responsible for transportation services between provinces and territories?

2. Create a map to show how you would travel from your community to Charlottetown, Prince Edward Island. Add your route and identify each mode of transportation you would use. Explain how each level of government would be involved in your trip.

How Do Governments Work Together to Help People in Need?

Governments work together to help people who are facing challenges. Some of these challenges are sudden, such as responding to natural disasters. Others are ongoing issues, such as homelessness and poverty.

Responding to Natural Disasters

In June 2013, communities in the southern part of Alberta were affected by flooding. All three levels of governments responded to this emergency.

Members of the Canadian Armed Forces worked alongside local officials to close roads during the flood in Alberta.

Municipal governments moved thousands of people from flooded areas. Local police and firefighters helped people escape the flooding. Some community buildings were made into shelters and meeting places.

During and after the flood, the provincial government also helped provide shelters. As well, it made emergency funds available to communities.

The federal government sent in hundreds of RCMP officers and members of the Canadian Armed Forces. They closed off damaged roads, rescued people, and helped pile sandbags to control flood water.

In High River, Alberta, all 13 000 community members had to leave their homes during the flood.

Helping People Who Are Homeless

To solve the issue of homelessness, all levels of government, private organizations, and individual citizens need to work together.

Provincial, territorial, and federal governments provide money to local governments and private organizations so that they can build affordable housing. The Wigwamen Waabnong housing project in Toronto is an example of many levels of government working together. All three levels of government contributed land or funds to this project.

Faith in Action

In 2014, students from Monsignor Morrison Catholic School in St. Thomas, Ontario, raised money through bake sales and hot chocolate sales to help local charities, such as the local women's shelter. They also served hot lunches to people in need.

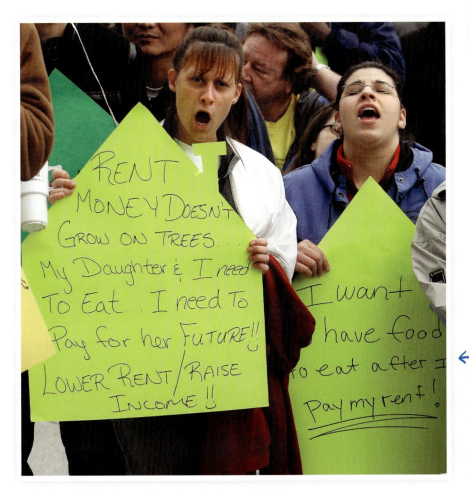

Many people think that the government is not doing enough to solve homelessness and poverty. These protestors in Alberta are calling on the provincial government to do more.

Explore and Apply

1. Explain the role that you think individual citizens have in solving issues such as homelessness.

2. If you had the opportunity to talk to your mayor, the premier, or the prime minister, what would you say about homelessness? Write a one-minute speech sharing your feelings and ideas.

Toolbox: Interpret and Analyze Information

Interpret and Analyze

When you interpret, you restate information in your own words to help you understand it. You might use sentences that start with "Another way of saying that is ..." or "The text is suggesting that ..."

When you analyze, you dig deeper to get to the heart of the matter. You take something apart to find out how it works. You ask probing questions to build a deeper understanding.

1. Determine which of the pieces of information that you gathered are relevant to your inquiry. Remember that your sources should be reliable and that you should use more than one source.

2. Identify important information and key ideas in graphs, charts, or maps.

3. Compare information from various sources. Look for patterns and connections. Ask yourself: What is the author's bias or perspective?

4. Develop a summary sentence or graphic organizer to show your analysis. Ask yourself: What new understanding of the topic or issue do I now have?

Colette's inquiry question was: What is being done to to help children living in poverty? She gathered this information from government websites.

In 2011 …

- 14 out of 100 children in Canada were living in poverty
- 14 out of 100 children in Ontario were living in poverty
- 12 out of 100 children in Toronto were living in poverty
- 25 out of 100 children in the Toronto Catholic District School Board were living in poverty

Poverty by the Numbers in Ontario

Over 1.7 million people live in poverty.

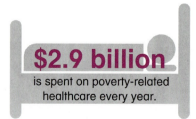
$2.9 billion is spent on poverty-related healthcare every year.

375 000 people rely on food banks.

More than 150 000 people are waiting for affordable housing.

Inquiry
Interpret and Analyze

Colette revised her inquiry question to probe more deeply: How do different levels of government support children in need in Toronto? She collected this information.

The Angel Foundation for Learning provides breakfast, snacks, and lunch to students in Toronto Catholic schools. This effort is supported by the Toronto Public Health department, as well as the provincial government. It serves food to about 30 000 students in over 100 schools.

Did You Know?
Research shows that students have improved attention spans and are more ready to learn when they have a healthy, nutritious, and filling breakfast.

Funding the Angel Foundation's Food Program

- 20 municipal and provincial governments
- 80 schools, parents, charities, and community sponsors

Colette researched where the Angel Foundation gets the money for its program. She summarized her findings in this pie chart. She was surprised that only 20 cents of every dollar came from the government.

Faith in Action
Grade 5 students at St. Patrick Elementary Catholic School in Brantford, Ontario, are working to help others under the name Grade5Can. They have made and sold bracelets, bookmarks, and hot chocolate. Grade5Can has helped the local Sunshine Foundation chapter, the Arnold Anderson Foundation, and the Juvenile Arthritis Foundation.

Explore and Apply

1. Interpret and analyze the information that Colette gathered. What new understanding of the topic or issue do you have now?

2. Find out about programs in your community to help children living in poverty. Create a summary statement to share your findings.

How Do Governments Work Together to Meet Environmental Challenges?

Protecting Our Water Supply

Governments often work together to build water treatment systems. They want to make sure Canadian citizens have safe drinking water. These systems also treat wastewater to protect the environment.

The federal government, the provincial government, and 14 municipal governments are cooperating to build a large water treatment project in Ontario. It will take water from Lake Huron and provide clean water to 500 000 people. The project was approved in 2009 and will cost about $350 million.

Providing clean water can be a challenge in small, rural communities. For example, many First Nations reserves have poor water treatment plants or none at all. Drinking water can be unsafe. The Assembly of First Nations and band councils work with the federal government to provide clean water on reserves.

Catholic Connection

In 2011, Cardinal Peter Turkson, of the Vatican, said that governments should provide citizens with access to water as part of the government's role in protecting the common good.

Thinking about Significance

In First Nations communities, for every 100 homes, 20 have unsafe drinking water. Some of these communities have been without safe water for decades. In 2013, the federal government passed a law to regulate the safety of drinking water in First Nations communities. Compare the information above to the rest of Canada, where only about 1 in 100 homes have to worry about the water coming from their taps. Note that in most Canadian communities, water safety is regulated by the province or territory.

This photo shows Iruwa Da Silva from the Grassy Narrows First Nation. She has health problems that may be caused by mercury in the drinking water on her reserve.

Cleaning Up Pollution

All levels of government take steps to protect the environment. Sometimes these efforts involve cleaning up pollution. These projects are often shared by more than one level of government.

For example, the federal government, Yukon's government, and local band councils are working together to clean up abandoned mine sites. About 900 small, contaminated mine sites were identified. As of 2013, more than 600 of these sites had been cleaned up.

This effort also involves large mine sites. Seven of these have been identified, including the Faro mine site northeast of Whitehorse. The Faro site has about 70 million tonnes of toxic mining waste. The cleanup of this site will take decades and will cost millions of dollars.

Community groups often help governments clean up and protect the environment. For example, each year, tens of thousands of Canadians take part in the Great Canadian Shoreline Cleanup. Volunteers in communities across Canada collect garbage along lakes, oceans, streams, and rivers.

The Faro lead–zinc mine was one of the biggest open-pit mines in the world. The tailings, or waste products, from the mine were kept in ponds that covered an area about 1 kilometre wide and 4 kilometres long. This aerial photo shows part of one tailing pond.

Explore and Apply

1. Mining companies that extract minerals from a mine often leave communities and regions to clean up the pollution they create. Governments are forced to step in. What do you think should be done to solve this problem?

2. Think of an issue connected to the environment. How do you think different levels of government can work together to solve the issue? Create a diagram or graphic organizer to show your ideas.

Spotlight on Managing the Great Lakes

Did You Know?

Josephine Mandamin, an Anishinabe Elder, has led walks around the Great Lakes. She and her supporters have walked more than 17 000 kilometres over six years. The goal of the group has been to draw attention to the problem of pollution in the Great Lakes, and the fact that we need to care for our water supply.

The Great Lakes are one of Canada's most important resources. We use these lakes for transportation, electrical power, recreation, and to provide drinking water.

About 30 million Canadians and Americans live in the region surrounding the Great Lakes. Unfortunately, this large population has led to the pollution of the Great Lakes. There are three main reasons for pollution in the Great Lakes:

- chemicals from industries
- waste from municipalities
- fuel from ships

Dealing with this pollution takes the cooperation of different levels of government. It also requires cooperation between Canada and the United States. An agreement between the two countries identified areas that are very polluted.

Areas of Concern in the Great Lakes, Canada, 2012

The federal government also signed an agreement with the Ontario government to cooperate in cleaning up the Great Lakes in Ontario. Together, the two governments have supported more than 800 projects. Many of these environmental projects involve building better facilities for treating wastewater.

Cleaning up the area can also involve moving large amounts of contaminated soil. For example, the Ontario government worked with the City of Windsor to remove soil along the banks of Turkey Creek. The soil had become polluted from years of industrial and residential waste. The soil was replaced with rocks, shrubs, and trees.

Pesticides used on crops can get washed away into rivers and lakes. The federal government is working with the farming industry to reduce pesticides. One strategy involves using lady bugs that feed on bugs that eat plants. For example, this species of lady bug eats soybean aphids. If left alone, the aphids would destroy soybean plants.

Foreign species, such as this Asian carp, can threaten local plants and animals. The Ontario Provincial Police, the Ontario Ministry of Natural Resources, the RCMP, and the federal Department of Oceans and Fisheries have worked together to create a plan to deal with this issue.

Explore and Apply

1. Explain why more than one level of government is needed to address environmental issues, such as cleaning up the Great Lakes.

2. Investigate one other foreign species that threatens the Great Lakes region. Communicate the results of your inquiry. Outline the threat and what is being done about it. Include an image of the species.

Pulling It Together

Father Mike Explains...

Pope Saint Gregory the Great wrote, "When we attend to the needs of those in want, we give them what is theirs, not ours. More than performing works of mercy, we are paying a debt of justice."

See

What works of mercy do you see in your community?

Reflect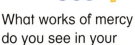

How do those works of mercy pay a debt of justice? What connections can you make?

Act

How can you contribute to the acts of mercy you see in your community? Work with a small group to outline some steps you can take.

How Do Governments Serve the Common Good?

My mom found a new job in Windsor. She found it with the help of the people at the Canada Employment Centre. Mom says that this experience has given her a new appreciation for what our governments do.

I learned that everyone may have times when they struggle and need help. My family has started to volunteer at the food bank. I want to do even more. I'm glad that our governments work together to help people. I think we can do a lot to help each other, too.

Colette

Governments can only do so much. It is important that community members also help themselves and one another. Organizations such as Habitat for Humanity work throughout Canada and the world to deal with issues such as poverty and homelessness. In this photo, a woman in Winnipeg, Manitoba, is helping her community members by working with others to build a home for a family in need.

Summarizing

Create the content for a web page titled "How Governments Work Together." Your purpose is to help new Canadians. On your page, summarize why governments work together and list some of the services that they provide. Include one example of governments working together.

Making Connections

Choose a photo or issue from the chapter that you can relate to or that you find interesting. How does it relate to your life, your family, or your community? Explain to a partner why this photo or topic is of interest to you.

Our Church says …

We are social beings and we need one another. The goal of social institutions, including governments, should be the protection and advancement of all people.

Chapter Inquiry

Choose one section of this chapter that deals with an issue. Interpret and analyze the information in that section. Develop a summary sentence or graphic organizer to show your analysis. You might use a graphic organizer such as the one shown here. Ask yourself: What new understanding of the topic or issue do I have now?

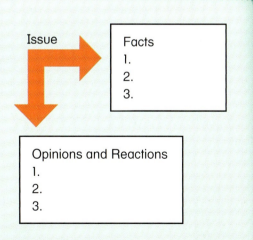

Chapter 4 Working Together

Chapter 5

The Rights and Responsibilities of Canadians

Big Question
How can we be active citizens in our community?

Learning Goals
- describe the major rights and responsibilities associated with citizenship in Canada
- evaluate evidence and draw conclusions
- create a plan that specifies actions that can be taken to address an issue

Canadians have the right to speak out freely for what they believe. This photo shows students protesting in Ottawa for equal education on First Nations reserves.

Hi, I'm Nicole.

I live in Sudbury, Ontario. My family moved here from Haiti before I was born.

Twelve years ago, my mom was a professor at the University of Haiti. One day, several students and professors were arrested for speaking out against the government. My parents decided that they didn't want to live in a country where people weren't free to speak about what they believed. Mom got a new job at Laurentian University in Sudbury.

Two years ago, my parents became Canadian citizens. My parents say that we are blessed to be living in a country where we have guaranteed rights and freedoms. I wonder what that means.

Our Faith

Saint John XXIII said ...

"Human dignity means that every person has the right to be active in public life and to do their part for the common good."

Peace on Earth (no. 26)

What Does It Mean to Be a Canadian Citizen?

A **citizen** is an official member of a country. Generally, if you are born in Canada, you are automatically a Canadian citizen. As a Canadian citizen, you have certain rights and freedoms. For example, you have the right to free speech and the right to live where you want in the country. You also have responsibilities, such as being loyal to Canada, obeying Canadian laws, and acting in a way that serves the common good.

People in Canada are free to express their opinions, practise their beliefs, and take part in cultural traditions. Canadian citizens are also free to take part in choosing their leaders. These freedoms do not exist in some parts of the world. There are countries where it is dangerous to have different beliefs or to speak out against the government.

Did You Know?
Until 1947, people in Canada were not Canadian citizens, but instead were British subjects. This meant that Canadians were governed by British law and the British monarch. In 1946, the *Canadian Citizenship Act, 1946,* was passed. It said that as of January 1, 1947, Canadian citizens were governed by the laws of Canada and owed loyalty to Canada.

Every Canada Day, millions of people show how proud they are to be Canadian. Each year, more than 150 000 immigrants become Canadian citizens. Canada's multicultural population is now made up of people from more than 200 different cultures. Most Canadians who were asked said that a good citizen accepts and welcomes all people.

Explore and Apply

1. Begin a t-chart to explore the strengths and challenges of Canada's multicultural population.

2. Write a short speech, explaining what being a Canadian citizen means to you.

What Are Our Rights as Canadians?

Thinking about Significance

One of the fundamental rights guaranteed by the Charter of Rights and Freedoms is the right to openly practise your religion. How is this right significant to a multicultural society like Canada?

Canadian rights are described in a part of the Constitution Act called the **Canadian Charter of Rights and Freedoms**. The Constitution is Canada's highest set of laws. New laws cannot take away any of the rights described in the Charter. The following are some of the rights guaranteed in the Charter:

Legal Rights
- To have life, liberty, and security
- To have a fair trial within a reasonable time
- To be held or imprisoned only if charged with a crime

Fundamental Freedoms
- To practise your religion
- To have and express your opinion
- To belong to and meet in peaceful groups

Equality Rights
- To live free from discrimination and prejudice

Enforcement Rights
- To go to court if any right guaranteed in the Charter is denied

Mobility Rights
- To enter or leave Canada as you wish
- To live anywhere in Canada

Language Rights
- To communicate and receive services provided by the Canadian government in either official language, French or English
- To have children in school taught in either of Canada's official languages

Democratic Rights
- To participate and vote in elections

88 Many Gifts Unit 1

Rights Beyond the Charter

Not all rights guaranteed to Canadians are in the Charter. For example, Aboriginal rights go beyond the rights in the Charter. Aboriginal rights include rights agreed to in the Canadian Constitution and treaties. **Treaties** are formal agreements between groups of people. Treaties were made between First Nations peoples and the federal government long ago. Aboriginal rights include the right to certain lands, the right to fish and hunt, and the right to practise Aboriginal culture.

While the Constitution recognizes Aboriginal rights, it does not describe exactly what these rights are. This can create challenges. When disagreements occur, the courts have to make a decision about what the Constitution means.

The Canadian government can limit Charter rights, as long as the limits are reasonable. For example, you have the right to free speech, but it is against the law to say anything that promotes hatred or violence. Governments are trying to use these limits to stop online bullying.

In this photo from December 2012, Andrea Landrey (left) speaks to other protestors. First Nations and Métis groups gathered at this rally in Windsor, Ontario, to protest government policies on the environment and Aboriginal rights.

Explore and Apply

1. Choose one Charter right and explain to a partner what you think it means. What connections can you make to this right?

2. Design a T-shirt to highlight a right that is guaranteed by the Charter. Explain to a partner the choices you made.

Toolbox: Evaluate and Draw Conclusions

Evaluating and Drawing Conclusions

As part of the inquiry process, it is important to make reasoned judgments. You first need to synthesize, question, and evaluate your research. This will help you to make informed, critical judgments. When you draw a conclusion or make a judgment, you take a position that can be supported based on the information you have gathered.

> 66 I am a Canadian, a free Canadian, free to speak without fear, free to worship God in my own way, free to stand for what I think right, free to oppose what I believe wrong, or free to choose those who shall govern my country. 99
>
> *John Diefenbaker, Prime Minister, 1957–1963*

Evaluating

1. Read over your research. Consider the different opinions or perspectives presented. What evidence, if any, supports those opinions or perspectives?

2. Identify the information that is most helpful in answering your inquiry question.

3. Identify the source of the information. Ask yourself: What makes this source trustworthy?

Nicole developed the following inquiry question: What does it mean to be a good Canadian citizen? She then gathered the following information.

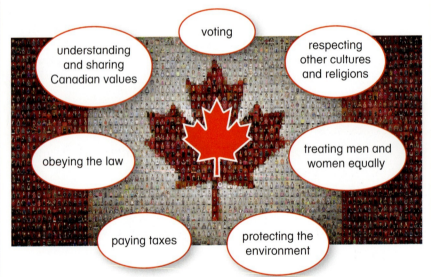

In 2011, the Institute for Canadian Citizenship conducted a survey called Canadians on Citizenship. Around 2300 Canadians were asked what makes someone a good citizen.

Inquiry
Evaluate and Draw Conclusions

The Oath of Citizenship

I swear (or affirm) that I will be faithful and bear true allegiance to Her Majesty Queen Elizabeth the Second, Queen of Canada, Her Heirs and Successors, and that I will faithfully observe the laws of Canada and fulfill my duties as a Canadian citizen.

> ... [new immigrants] will take on all the same responsibilities as other citizens—obeying our laws, paying taxes, etc. I always tell new citizens that citizenship is a fixed menu, not a self-serve buffet where you can pick and choose. Once you are adopted in the family of your fellow citizens, you accept the good with the bad.

Adrienne Clarkson, Governor General, 1999–2005

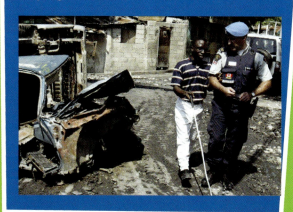

Many Canadians believe that a good citizen is willing to serve Canada by joining the Armed Forces. Many also feel that it is important for Canada to play a role in peacekeeping around the world. In this photo, a peacekeeper is helping a citizen in Haiti.

Drawing Conclusions

1. Make connections between the pieces of information. Compare the various perspectives and opinions. Think about your own opinion.
2. Develop statements to summarize your evaluation.
3. Use these statements to draw conclusions you can support.

Explore and Apply

1. Evaluate the information that Nicole has gathered. Write a summary statement and then draw a conclusion in response to her inquiry question.
2. Find a current news story that connects to Nicole's inquiry. Write a summary sentence that describes the connection.

What Are the Responsibilities of Citizenship?

As Canadians, we have rights. Along with these rights come the following responsibilities:

- obeying the law
- supporting oneself and one's family to the best of one's ability
- serving on a jury during a court case, if one is asked to do so
- voting in elections
- helping others in the community

Part of being a good citizen is understanding, respecting, preserving, and enjoying Canadian heritage and the environment. For example, all Canadians must understand and respect the place of both the French and British in Canadian history. Canadian citizens must also understand, respect, and honour the relationship and agreements made between the Government of Canada and Canada's Aboriginal peoples.

People who wish to become Canadian citizens must take an Oath of Citizenship. If they are between the ages of 18 and 54, they must also pass a test.

Catholic Connection

Our Catholic faith can help us fulfill our responsibilities as active citizens. For example, the Ontario Catholic Graduate Expectations require students to promote a just, peaceful, and compassionate society.

This photo shows a group of Canadians exploring Mitlenatch Island, British Columbia. They are learning about its history and ecosystems.

Active Citizenship

Many people believe that it is the responsibility of a good citizen to be an active citizen. Being an active citizen means taking interest in the issues that affect the community. When asked, most Canadians say that it is the responsibility of Canadian citizens to care for others.

Volunteering is one way that people are active in their communities. Volunteers can take action to address social and environmental issues in their community. When they do so, they serve the common good.

Did You Know?
In 2010, more than half of all Canadians did some volunteer work. Young people and people who were active in their faith were more likely to volunteer their time.

In this photo, a volunteer helps raise money at a concert in Winnipeg, Manitoba. The concert was to benefit an organization called War Child Canada, which helps children around the world affected by war.

Faith in Action
St. Anne Catholic Elementary School in Richmond Hill, Ontario, has a Social Justice Committee. Students on the committee volunteer their time to organize the St. Vincent de Paul Christmas Basket Drive. Students fill Christmas baskets for families in need with household and personal care items, as well as with gifts and toys.

In this photo, a volunteer prepares to put a band around the leg of a scarlet tanager. Volunteers at the Haldimand Bird Observatory near Cayuga, Ontario, band hundreds of birds every spring and fall. This helps them find out about the migration patterns of many different species of birds.

Explore and Apply

1. Should all Canadians have to take an oath of citizenship? Support your opinion.
2. Create a poster that will encourage Canadian citizens to learn about and practise their responsibilities.

Spotlight on the Order of Canada

The Order of Canada is an award that recognizes Canadian citizens. Citizens receive the award for service to Canada or the world. Queen Elizabeth II created this award in 1967. The motto of the Order of Canada is "They Desire a Better Country."

There are three levels of the Order of Canada. More than 6000 people have been honoured with the Order of Canada.

Member of the Order of Canada	Officer of the Order of Canada	Companion of the Order of Canada
People who receive this award have served a community or group.	People who receive this award have served Canada, or the world, with a high degree of excellence and distinction.	People who receive this award have served Canada, or the world, with the highest degree of excellence and distinction.

Lucia Kowaluk, from Montréal, Québec, became a Member of the Order of Canada in 2013. She helped create affordable housing, opened drop-in centres for the homeless, and saved green spaces and heritage sites. She said, "All I've ever done is see something that enrages me because it's not just, and then do something about it."

Joy Kogawa became a Member of the Order of Canada in 1986. She was recognized as a writer and poet. The award also acknowledged her role in encouraging the Canadian government to apologize to Japanese Canadians. The apology was for the unfair treatment they received during World War II. During the war, thousands of Japanese families were forced from their homes and into camps.

Phil Fontaine received the award of Officer of the Order of Canada in 2012. He is the former chief of the Sagkeeng First Nation. He served as grand chief of the Assembly of Manitoba Chiefs and was national chief of the Assembly of First Nations. He has been active in pursuing fairer treatment for First Nations peoples in Canada.

Explore and Apply

1. Do you think it is important that a country has a way of recognizing people who have made great contributions? Is it necessary to be rewarded for doing good acts? Support your answers.

2. Choose another person who has received the Order of Canada. Find a photo and at least five points of information that show why that person deserves the award. Add your page to a class digital presentation.

How Are Elections Both a Right and a Responsibility?

Participating in an election is a right guaranteed by the Canadian Charter. Every Canadian citizen 18 years of age or older has the right to vote in elections.

Canadians under 18 years of age can still take part in the election process. They can learn about the different issues and where different parties stand on these issues. Young people can then support a particular viewpoint by discussing the issues with friends and family.

Canadians vote by marking a ballot and placing it in a ballot box. People in some countries around the world do not have the right to vote. In other countries, the voting process may be subject to fraud or abuse.

Young people can learn about the election process by participating in school council elections. How can participating in a school council election prepare students to be active citizens?

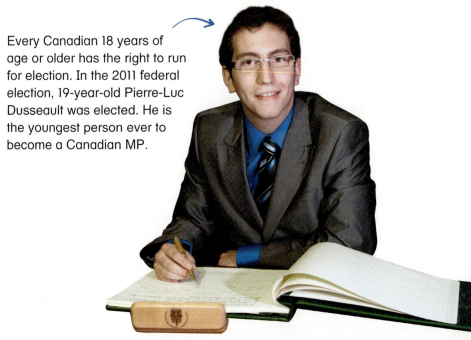

Every Canadian 18 years of age or older has the right to run for election. In the 2011 federal election, 19-year-old Pierre-Luc Dusseault was elected. He is the youngest person ever to become a Canadian MP.

Taking part in elections is a responsibility of citizenship. When people vote, they make a statement about what they believe. A vote sends a message to the community that there is support for different people and different ideas.

Voters also have a responsibility to know why they are supporting a certain person or party. There are many opportunities for voters to learn about the issues. Candidates often create pamphlets or make speeches to promote their ideas. There are also meetings that voters can attend to listen to candidates share ideas.

Voters should ask themselves what they believe is important. This way, they can evaluate each candidate and vote for the candidate whose ideas are most like their own.

Getting to Know the Candidates

Before deciding who to vote for, Canadians need to ask the following questions: Who are the candidates? What experience do they have? What do they say about different issues? How have they acted in the past in regard to different issues? Do their ideas and actions reflect the values that the voter wants in a leader?

Catholic Connection

In 2007, the Ontario Conference of Catholic Bishops created a document that says that governments are in power because voters put them there. The bishops say it is voters, not the government, who are responsible for the direction in which society moves.

Before elections, candidates from different parties gather to speak and share their ideas with voters. This photo shows candidates for the federal government taking part in a debate in London, Ontario.

Explore and Apply

1. Think about a time when you and your friends made a decision. How did you decide?

2. Think of an issue that you feel is important in your community. List questions that you would like to ask the municipal candidates. For each question, write the responses that best reflect your beliefs about the issue.

Toolbox: Create an Action Plan

An action plan is a step-by-step strategy for completing a project. It is created before the project is started. Creating and following an action plan make it easier to keep a project on schedule and complete it successfully.

An action plan outlines what steps need to be taken, when they need to be taken, and who needs to take them. Use these steps to create an action plan:

1. Write a sentence to describe the issue that you hope to address.
2. Write a sentence to explain your goal.
3. If necessary, collect further information on the issue.
4. Decide on the steps that need to be followed to reach your goal.
5. State when each step needs to be completed and who is responsible for completing it.

Remember to evaluate and revise the plan as you work on it. Check that you are on track. Often, unexpected events can mean that you have to make changes to your plan.

Faith in Action

On November 8, 2013, a powerful storm destroyed large parts of the Philippines. Students at Sacred Heart School in Espanola, Ontario, wanted to help. They held a hat day and bake sale, raising more than $850 for the Red Cross for relief in the Philippines.

Think about the steps you would need to include in an action plan for organizing a track and field event. From this photo, what do you think organizers had to do before the event? What will they have to do during and after it?

The church that Nicole attends donates Easter hampers to families in need. Nicole and her friends Jack and Li Min decide to hold a bake sale to support this program. This is their action plan.

Fun Run Bake Sale, April 20th

The issue	The church Easter hamper program needs funds.			
Goal	Raise $500 by organizing a bake sale during the school's fun run.			
Action steps	Create 40 posters and post them at school and church.	Bake 12 dozen cupcakes, 10 cakes, and 100 cookies.	Deliver the baked goods, the table, and a sign for the table.	Work at the baked goods table at the fun run.
Who is responsible?	Jack and his brother Matt	Nicole, Li Min, Jack, and their parents	Li Min and her dad in her parents' van	Nicole, Jack, Li Min, and Nicole's mom
When will the step be completed?	April 14th	April 19th	April 20th, 8:45 a.m.	April 20th, 9 a.m. to 2 p.m.
Materials and resources needed	poster boards, felt pens, computer, printer, tape	baking supplies, ovens, help from adults	van, a table from the church, a sign for the table	cash box, change, signs
Possible obstacles	getting permission to put up the posters; delivering the posters	cost of supplies; place to store all the baked goods	none	Jack may not be able to make it because of dance class.

Decide on a way to effectively communicate your action plan. Your communication tool will let people know what steps need to be taken, as well as who is responsible for taking actions. This will help keep your project on track.

Explore and Apply

1. Explain why creating an action plan would make it easier to succeed at a project. What would be some of the challenges of working on a project without an action plan?

2. Think of a project that you could take on to help address an issue in your school or community. Create an action plan for your project. How will other people be included?

Thinking about Interrelationships

Sometimes the government cannot solve social and environmental issues without the help of citizens. What examples can you think of where government and citizens have worked together effectively to address an issue?

Chapter 5 The Rights and Responsibilities of Canadians

Pulling It Together

Father Mike Explains...

Every one of us has the opportunity to have a positive effect on our communities. In their 1995 guide for Catholic voters, the Catholic bishops of England and Wales said, "A society [that has no] regard for the common good would be unpleasant and dangerous to live in, as well as unjust to those it excluded."

See

Not everyone who can vote chooses to vote in an election. Why would someone choose not to vote?

Reflect

How does taking seriously our responsibility to vote connect to the common good?

Act

Create a TV or radio ad that encourages people to vote.

How Can I Be a Responsible Citizen?

Our family is very active in Sudbury. We help at the local food bank and assist new immigrants at the Friendship Centre.

My brothers and I talk about politics with our parents. Dad says it's important to know what the government is doing. We have a voice. Mom says that we should never take for granted our right to vote. There are people in other parts of the world who are willing to fight and die for that right.

I'm glad we live in Canada. One day, I want to be a politician so I can be part of making laws to help others.

Nicole

In this photo, volunteers help at a food bank. Hundreds of thousands of people across Canada depend on food banks every day. Think about how citizens can use their voting power to solve problems such as poverty and hunger.

Many Gifts Unit 1

Summarizing

Create a picture book that will help children from other countries understand Canadian citizenship. Use words and pictures to present the rights and freedoms that Canadians have. Your picture book should summarize the information you learned in this chapter.

Making Connections

Choose a group or a person who is active in making your community better. Create a short video or interview to celebrate this group or person.

Saint John XXIII said ...

 Human dignity means that every person has the right to be active in public life and to do their part for the common good.

Peace on Earth (no. 26)

Chapter Inquiry

Revisit the Big Question at the beginning of the chapter: How can we be active citizens in our community?

Gather information from this chapter and other sources to answer this question. What perspectives on this question have you found? Organize your information.

Use your information to evaluate and draw conclusions. Record your conclusions and share them with a small group.

Unit Inquiry

An Action Plan for the Common Good

As an active Canadian citizen, you will complete an inquiry project, investigating a social or environmental issue in your community. Your inquiry will result in an action plan. Your action plan will

- provide citizens and government with steps to address the issue and benefit the common good
- present a possible solution
- identify any challenges or obstacles
- be flexible, allowing for changes in the steps

Formulate Questions

Review the chapters and select an issue to research. Think about what you already know about the issue. Start a KWL chart.

Share your questions with other students, and then revise or add to your chart. Review the information on your chart. Develop an inquiry question to guide your research.

Checklist

My question will

- ☑ guide my research
- ☑ help me to think about the issue
- ☑ help me to understand the roles of the people involved

Gather and Organize Information

Review relevant information in the chapters for this unit. Look for additional sources of information that will help you to answer your inquiry question. Check the library, the Internet, magazines, and newspapers. Organize the information that you gather from the different sources. You may choose to use a graphic organizer. Organizing information can help you begin to interpret and analyze it.

Review the information that you have gathered and organized. Decide whether more information is needed. If so, where will you look?

Checklist
I will

- ☑ identify resources I can use
- ☑ check that I have enough information to answer my question
- ☑ determine the accuracy and reliability of the sources
- ☑ organize my information in a meaningful way

Interpret and Analyze Information

Reread the information that you have gathered about the issue. Identify the key points or ideas in each piece of information. Extract information from maps, graphs, charts, and diagrams. Create a summary statement for each piece of information.

Make connections between ideas. Make sure you understand the importance of the issue from the perspective of different groups of people. You may want to organize your information to show relationships between pieces of information. What new understanding do you have?

Checklist
I will

- ☑ determine what is important
- ☑ use my own words to summarize my research
- ☑ make connections to the issue
- ☑ consider the perspective of an author or source
- ☑ identify the level of government most involved in addressing the issue
- ☑ identify any new understanding I have

Unit Inquiry

Checklist

I will

- ☑ consider different perspectives on the issue
- ☑ consider the evidence that supports different options or perspectives
- ☑ draw conclusions based on my evaluation
- ☑ determine what obstacles or challenges people might face in addressing the issue

Evaluate and Draw Conclusions

Evaluate the information and draw conclusions to answer these questions: How could the issue be resolved? Who would be involved in resolving the issue, including citizens and people in different levels of government? What obstacles might they face?

As you develop answers to these questions, remember to make judgments that you can defend based on evidence you have gathered. Finally, draw conclusions about how citizens and government can work together to solve the issue. Your conclusions will help you create an action plan.

Communicate the Results of Your Inquiry

Now it is time to communicate the results of your inquiry. You will do so by creating an action plan to deal with the issue. You might use an organizer like the one below.

Checklist

I will

- ☑ create an action plan
- ☑ share information and conclusions in an interesting way

I will include in my action plan

- ☑ a statement about the issue
- ☑ the goal in taking action
- ☑ the obstacles that I see and how they can be overcome

The issue				
The goal				
Action steps	1	2	3	4
Who is responsible for each step?				
When will the step be completed?				
Materials/resources needed				
Possible challenges/ obstacles				
How will I know that the goal has been achieved?				

Once your action plan is complete, have a partner look it over to make sure that everything is clear.

Share your action plan with your class. You might do so in the role of a social activist or environmentalist, a mayor, a band council member, an MP, or an MPP. Or you might create a newspaper article, webcast, or TV interview to share your action plan.

What documents will support your action plan? Consider including maps, petitions, diagrams, photos, and graphic organizers.

Extend Your Learning

Consider who will be affected by your action plan. How do you think people's lives might be changed?

Reflect on Your Learning

Check that you have successfully completed each part of the inquiry process. Think about what you have learned. Ask yourself the following questions:

- What part of the project shows my best work?
- What could I have done differently?
- What did I learn through the process?
- What did I learn about active citizenship and government?
- How could my action plan contribute to the common good?

Unit 2
First Nations and European Explorers

We study Canada's past to understand how our country came to be. In this unit, you will learn about First Nations peoples in eastern Canada and their lives before Europeans came to this land. You will also learn about the lives of Europeans who came to Canada. You will investigate how First Nations peoples and Europeans interacted with each other.

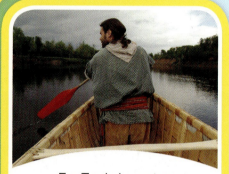

Fur Trade in eastern Canada, 1500s–1713

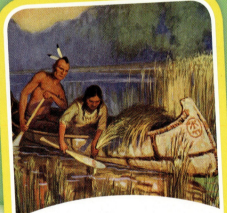

First Nations Peoples in eastern Canada, Before 1600

Our Faith

Pope Paul VI said ...

"Nation [must] meet nation, as brothers and sisters, as children of God. In this mutual understanding and friendship, in this sacred communion, we must also begin to work together to build the common future of the human race."

On the Development of Peoples (no. 43)

Legend
- area that would become Canada
- area that would become the United States
- community

0   240 km

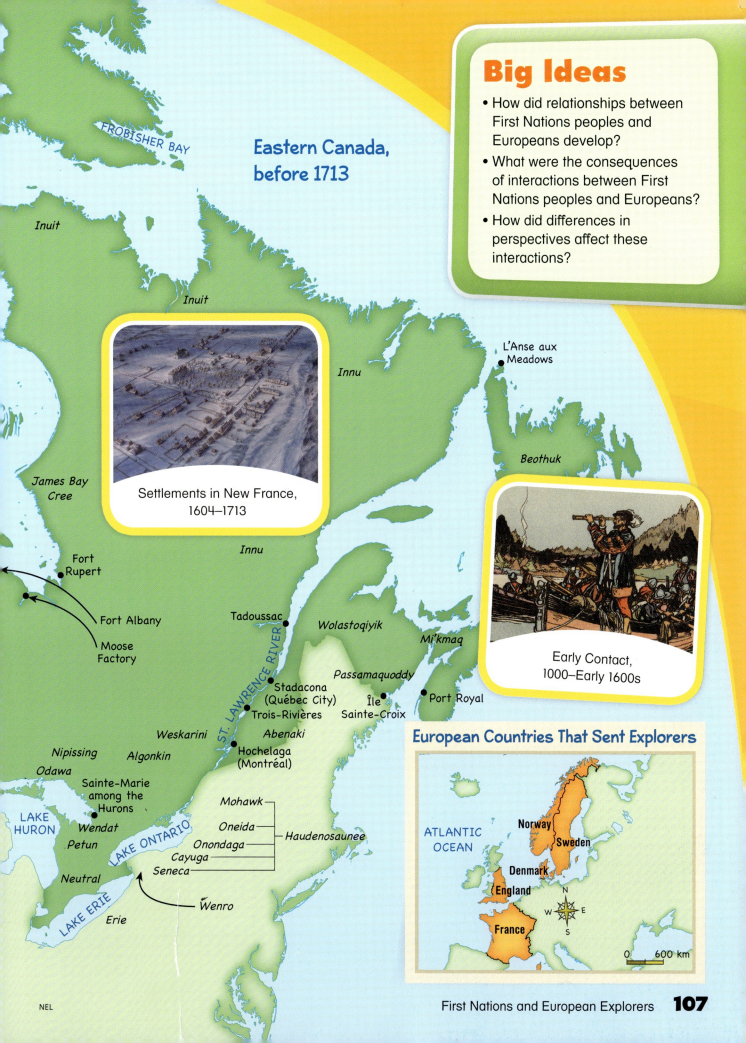

Thinking about "Canada" in the Past

In this unit, you will learn about eastern Canada before 1713. When we refer to Canada and use place names, we are generally using their present-day names. It is important to remember that before 1867, Canada as a country did not exist. It was home to First Nations peoples and Inuit long before Europeans came here.

When Europeans arrived, the lives of First Nations peoples in eastern Canada began to change. Both groups had to find ways to live with and respect each other. Together, First Nations peoples and Europeans helped shape the country that Canada is today.

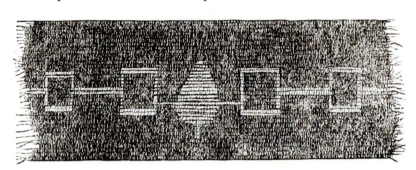

This wampum belt provides a record of the Great Law of Peace.

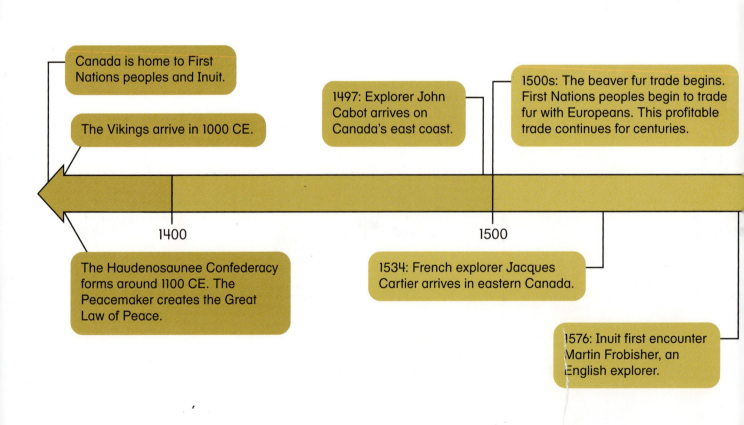

Canada is home to First Nations peoples and Inuit.

The Vikings arrive in 1000 CE.

1497: Explorer John Cabot arrives on Canada's east coast.

1500s: The beaver fur trade begins. First Nations peoples begin to trade fur with Europeans. This profitable trade continues for centuries.

1400

1500

The Haudenosaunee Confederacy forms around 1100 CE. The Peacemaker creates the Great Law of Peace.

1534: French explorer Jacques Cartier arrives in eastern Canada.

1576: Inuit first encounter Martin Frobisher, an English explorer.

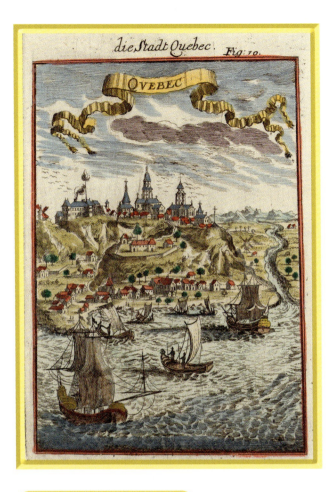

This early painting shows the beginning of the settlement at Québec City.

This postage stamp was issued in 2001 to remember and honour the signing of a treaty between First Nations peoples and the French.

- 1603: French mapmaker Samuel de Champlain arrives in eastern Canada. Wendat guides help him map eastern Canada.
- 1608: The French establish a settlement at what was once a First Nations village.
- 1701: First Nations and the French sign the Great Peace of Montréal.
- 1611: Missionaries begin to arrive in New France.
- 1713: Much of New France comes under the rule of England as part of a peace agreement.
- 1610: English explorer Henry Hudson sails to northern Canada.
- 1670: The English create the Hudson's Bay Company.

First Nations and European Explorers

Getting Started

Before learning about something new, it is important to think about what you already know. This helps you make personal connections to the topic. Then you can generate questions about what you want to find out or what you still wonder about.

Here are some questions and thoughts that Shamina had about First Nations peoples and Europeans in early Canada.

My Questions and Thoughts

- Who were some of the First Nations peoples in Eastern Canada? How did they live? How were First Nations communities similar? How were they different? I wonder how my community today is different from those long ago.

- Why did early European explorers come to Canada? How did they interact with First Nations peoples? How did they communicate? I think communicating with each other would have been a real challenge.

- What was the fur trade? Who was involved? What impact did it have on different people and on the environment?

- Why did Europeans start settlement communities? How did settlements impact the lives of First Nations peoples? I wonder what it was like to live in early settlements. I think life must have been really hard.

Explore and Apply

1. What do you already know about First Nations peoples and early European explorers and settlers?

2. List any questions you have.

Father Mike Explains …

Pope Paul VI said, "We have inherited from past generations and we have benefited from the work of our contemporaries." He was explaining human **solidarity**, or unity between people. People and cultures differ, but we are all humans. We can and should learn from each other.

When we study the interactions among and between First Nations peoples and Europeans in early Canada, we can understand that different people have different viewpoints and these affect the way they act. Yet, we also see how much they have in common. History helps us develop a sense of respect for people, encourages us to understand others, and leads us to develop a greater spirit of openness and welcome toward all. We share one world and are involved with one another in our progress toward God.

Looking Ahead to the Unit Inquiry

For the Unit Inquiry, you will become a young archaeologist. It is your job to investigate the interactions between groups of people in early Canada. For example, you might decide to investigate the meeting between the people of Stadacona and Jacques Cartier or the relationship between the Wendat and French fur traders.

You will then research to gather historical evidence. Some information will come from primary sources, such as artifacts and journal accounts. Other information will come from secondary sources, such as articles, photos of reconstructions, and paintings created after this time period.

Using your collection of historical evidence, you will

- reflect on how people interacted with each other
- think about the lives of people after contact
- draw conclusions about the effects of interaction between the groups of people

You will then communicate the findings of your inquiry. See pages 200 to 203 for more information on the Unit Inquiry.

Chapter 6

First Nations Peoples in Eastern Canada
Before 1600

Big Question
What does community mean to First Nations peoples?

Learning Goals
- identify and compare some First Nations groups in early Canada
- formulate questions
- describe interactions among and between First Nations peoples

Elizabeth Doxtater is a modern artist who created this work of art to represent the Haudenosaunee Confederacy and the Great Law of Peace.

Hi, I'm Nick.

I'm a member of the Oneida First Nation. I live near Brantford, Ontario, in the Six Nations community.

I love listening to the stories that my grandmother tells about my ancestors. They were one of the first peoples to live here. They lived here long before there were supermarkets, hospitals, airports, and schools. My ancestors formed communities where they cared for each other and shared everything they had.

I wonder how other First Nations peoples lived long ago. Were their communities like those of my ancestors?

Our Faith

Saint John XXIII said ...

"The family is the first essential cell of human society."

112 Many Gifts Unit 2

How Do We Learn about First Nations Peoples?

We learn about First Nations peoples from their rich oral tradition. An **oral tradition** is the passing of knowledge, history, and culture from one generation to the next through spoken words. Elders help to pass on First Nations knowledge by telling stories to children and other community members.

We also learn about the lives of First Nations peoples from artifacts. Artifacts provide us with clues about the past. Artifacts are primary sources and can include tools, weapons, clothing, jewellery, and toys.

Catholic Connection

Stories about Jesus were shared through oral tradition before they were written down.

These tools are at least 3000 years old. They were found in New Brunswick and include slate knives and stone weights for fishing nets.

These pieces of jewellery, made from shells and stones, are more than 800 years old. First Nations peoples living in the southern regions of Ontario and Québec may have made these, or they may have traded for them. When archaeologists find artifacts like these, they ask themselves questions such as the following: Who made these items and why? How did people living in this region get shells from sea animals whose habitats were much farther away?

Explore and Apply

1. What clues do the artifacts on this page give you about the lives of First Nations peoples long ago?
2. Start a KWL chart on First Nations peoples. Add to the chart, including new questions, as you work through this unit.

Chapter 6 First Nations Peoples in Eastern Canada

Why Was the Environment Important to First Nations Peoples?

First Nations peoples living in what is now eastern Canada relied on the environment for the resources they needed. The land and all its resources were gifts of the Creator. First Nations peoples greatly respected these gifts. They took only what they needed.

First Nations peoples led different ways of life depending on their environment. Some nations farmed and built villages in which they lived for many years. Other nations moved as the seasons changed. They knew where animals, fish, and plants were at particular times of the year. They travelled to hunt and gather them.

First Nations peoples used plants and animals for a variety of needs and wants.

Thinking about Interrelationships

Before the arrival of the Europeans in the 1500s, First Nations peoples in Canada did not have access to certain materials or manufactured goods, such as iron knives or pots. Everything they needed had to be found in their immediate environment. Consider how this affected their relationship with nature.

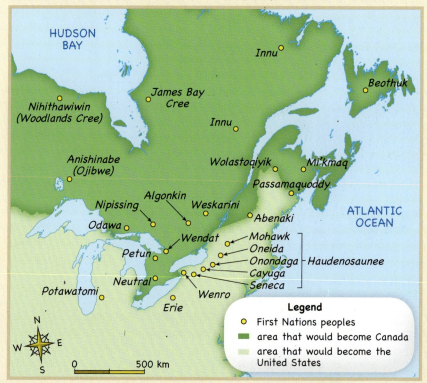

This map shows the approximate locations of some of the First Nations peoples who lived in eastern Canada before Canada even existed. Information about where these peoples lived is based partly on archaeological findings. However, it is important to remember that the territory of many First Nations covered a large area. For example, the Mi'kmaq travelled throughout what is now New Brunswick, Nova Scotia, and Prince Edward Island.

Food

In the Great Lakes–St. Lawrence region, the rich soil and climate were suitable for farming. The Haudenosaunee grew corn, beans, squash, and other crops. They tapped trees for maple syrup and gathered wild berries, mushrooms, and herbs. They also hunted and fished.

In northern areas, the land was rockier. The soil was less fertile and the temperature was cooler. First Nations peoples here, such as the Anishinabe, hunted in the forests, fished the lakes and rivers, and gathered wild rice from the marshy shores. **Wild rice** is a grain that grows naturally, without being farmed. It was an important food staple to First Nations peoples in the Great Lakes region.

In Atlantic Canada, First Nations peoples hunted in the forests and along the coasts. They fished the oceans and rivers. They also gathered berries and the eggs of wild birds. Even though the Wolastoqiyik were mainly hunters and gatherers, they also grew crops. They lived on the fertile land along the St. John River in New Brunswick.

Shelter

First Nations peoples who lived in villages built longhouses. **Longhouses** are solid, permanent homes made of wood and bark. Many related families lived in each longhouse.

Here and Now
Today, you can still find areas where wild rice grows naturally, but it is also being farmed and exported to other countries. Unfortunately, wild rice beds are threatened by the logging industry and pollution.

First Nations peoples still harvest wild rice as they did years ago. Wild rice is also called *manomin*, water rice, or blackbird oats.

This reconstructed longhouse is at the site of what was once a village of the Wendat, near Milton, Ontario.

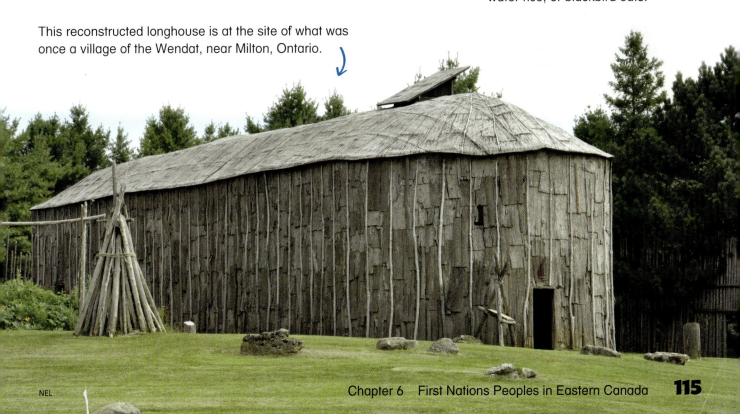

Some First Nations peoples who moved as the seasons changed lived in temporary homes called *wigwams*. **Wigwams** are dome- or cone-shaped structures made with a wooden frame covered with animal skins or tree bark. One or more families lived together in these smaller shelters.

Clothing

First Nations peoples made clothing from the skins of animals in their environment. For example, the Mi'kmaq wore loose robes of caribou or moose fur, with leggings made from seal hide. They wore moccasins made of moosehide or sealskin.

Some First Nations peoples, such as the Algonkin and Anishinabe, built shelters similar to this reconstructed wigwam. Reconstructions are based on information from oral stories and archaeologists' findings. Compare the wigwam to the longhouse.

These traditional Wendat moccasins were made from animal hides, moosehair, and other materials. These were made in the 1800s, but they are similar to those from earlier periods (before the Europeans arrived).

This traditional Innu coat was made in the late 1700s from caribou hides. Dyes made from plants were used to create the design. The Innu sewed pieces of leather together with a bone needle and animal sinew.

Explore and Apply

1. What natural resources do you think First Nations peoples living in your area depended on?

2. Choose one of the items not covered in this section from the web at the top of page 114 (transportation, tools, medicine, weapons). What questions do you have about how First Nations peoples used natural resources to fulfill that need or want? Create a research plan to answer one of your questions.

Who Belonged to a First Nations Community?

First Nations communities were organized by kinship. **Kinship** is the tie between people who are related through blood or marriage. Communities depended on everyone working together and being respectful, cooperative, and generous.

Elders

Elders were (and still are) knowledge keepers and teachers in their communities. From Elders, children learn about their history and traditions. They also learn about their responsibilities to their communities and to have respect for all Creation. Elders advise leaders so that wise decisions are made for the community.

Artist Daphne Odjig created this painting called *Homage to Grandfather: Belonging* in 1980. Odjig is an artist of Odawa–Potawatomi–English heritage. Her creativity was greatly influenced by her grandfather.

Men

Among most First Nations peoples, men generally hunted and fished, especially large mammals such as moose and bear. They made sure the whole community had enough food. Men built shelters for their families and traded with other First Nations peoples. When necessary, men fought in wars against other First Nations to protect or expand their community. In farming communities, men cleared land and prepared it for planting.

This photo shows some of the artifacts a Mi'kmaq family would use to gather and prepare food. What connections can you make to these items?

Women

First Nations Women generally prepared the animals that the men hunted and roasted the meat over an open fire. They preserved some of the meat by hanging it on wooden racks over a smoky fire.

First Nations Women also hunted small birds and mammals, such as partridges and rabbits. They gathered roots, berries, nuts, and mushrooms, as well as eggs from wild birds. Women in farming communities planted and harvested crops.

Children

The entire First Nations community cared for children. Children learned practical skills that prepared them for life as adults. Boys played games that taught them how to hunt and fish. They learned these and other skills from their fathers, uncles, and grandfathers. Girls learned skills, such as preparing food and making clothing, from their mothers, aunts, and grandmothers.

This artwork was created by Father Francisco Creuxio in 1664. It shows Haudenosaunee women preparing food. Would you consider this a primary or secondary source? Support your answer.

Daphne Odjig created these paintings, *Homage to Grandfather: Learning* (right) and *Homage to Grandfather: Listening*. What do these paintings suggest about the relationship between children and adults?

Explore and Apply

1. Why do you think it was important for everyone in a First Nations community to contribute to the community's well-being?

2. Create a graphic organizer to show the roles in a First Nations community.

How Did Communities Make Decisions?

First Nations communities usually made decisions through consensus. They carefully considered the well-being of the whole community. They also respected traditions, the environment, and each other.

Talking Circles

Many First Nations peoples used talking circles to reach consensus. They still use talking circles today. The circle is an important symbol to First Nations peoples. It has no beginning or end and no marked place for a leader or followers. Each member of the circle belongs and is equal.

Before a talking circle begins, some First Nations peoples perform a smudging ceremony. They burn sacred plants, such as sweet grass, sage, or cedar. **Smudging** cleanses people so that they can take part in the talking circle with honesty and a clear mind. A sacred object from nature, such as a stick, stone, or feather, is then passed around. The person holding the object speaks while everyone else in the circle listens respectfully. Anyone who does not wish to speak can pass the object forward. Silence is respected.

Faith in Action

The Catholic District School Board of Eastern Ontario has an anti-bullying policy that uses talking circles to resolve conflict. The school board believes that talking circles build positive relationships and encourage communication, taking responsibility, and healing.

Did You Know?

Sage was considered a women's medicine by some First Nations peoples. Sage gave women strength, wisdom, and focus and also drove away negative energy.

This photo shows Wendat Elder Ohney Maher performing a smudging ceremony in Québec City.

Explore and Apply

1. Do you think a talking circle would be an effective tool to resolve conflict in schools? Why, or why not?
2. Create an action plan for dealing with a school issue. As part of your plan, include using a talking circle to find out how different people feel about the issue. Share with the class how the talking circle helped you reach consensus.

Spotlight on the Wendat

Here is a more in-depth look at how the Wendat lived. As you read, compare what you learn about the Wendat with what you have already learned.

The Wendat lived on fertile land, close to forests. Summers were hot and winters were cold and snowy.

The fertile soil and the climate allowed the Wendat to farm. This meant that they did not have to travel far for food. Instead, they lived in one place and built villages. Some villages had as many as 1000 people.

The Wendat usually built their villages near water so that they could catch fish, water their crops, and travel by canoe. Villages were also located on raised ground for defence.

This artwork of a Wendat village was created by Charles William Jefferys for a book of illustrations published in 1942.

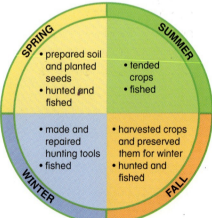

This diagram shows some of the food-related activities that the Wendat planned around the seasons.

Food

Similar to many First Nations peoples who farmed, the Wendat men cleared the land. The women planted, tended, and harvested crops. The main crops were corn, beans, and squash. These three crops were known as The Three Sisters.

Men hunted deer and other animals in the forests and fished in lakes and streams. Often, they hunted in groups and shared the meat with the whole community. They showed respect for the animal by using every part of it, including using the fur for clothing.

Shelter

Each Wendat village had many longhouses, in which several clans lived together. About six related families lived in each longhouse. Longhouses were constructed from wood and bark.

Clothing

In summer, men wore loincloths and women wore skirts. In winter, men and women wore leggings, shirts, and fur robes for extra warmth. They also wore moccasins.

Women made clothing from the skins of deer, beaver, rabbit, and other animals. They decorated the clothing with porcupine quills, shells, feathers, and beads. They crushed flowers, fruits, and berries to dye the clothing.

Decision Making

The Wendat grouped themselves into eight clans. Everyone in a clan was related to the same female ancestor. Each clan was led by a Clan Mother and elected male chiefs. There were two types of clan chiefs: civil chiefs and war chiefs. Civil chiefs were concerned with daily life. War chiefs were in charge of military action and defence.

Clan chiefs represented their clans at village council meetings, where they made decisions for the whole community. The council met often and made final decisions only when everyone reached consensus, or agreed.

This picture shows part of the inside of a longhouse. What might be some challenges for many people living together in one longhouse?

Clans

In some First Nations, such as the Wendat, clan members are related through the mother's side. In other First Nations, such as the Anishinabe, clan members are related through the father's side.

Explore and Apply

1. Compare the ways you depend on the environment to the ways the Wendat depended on the environment.
2. Create a model or illustration of a Wendat village to show some of the roles of men and women.

Spotlight on the Innu

Catholic Connection

The Bible has stories that teach respect for God's gifts. After Jesus fed thousands of people with five loaves of bread and two fish, he said to his disciples, "Gather up the fragments left over, so that nothing may be lost." (John 6:12, NRSV)

Did You Know?

The Innu made tea using pine needles. This tea helped prevent colds and infections during the long winters.

Here is a more in-depth look at how the Innu lived. As you read, compare what you learn about the Innu with what you have just learned about the Wendat.

Where the Innu lived was rocky and not suitable for farming. The land was also surrounded by forests. In summer, the Innu lived near the coast of the Atlantic Ocean. In winter, they moved inland. The climate was much colder than the region in which the Wendat lived.

In 1875, William Raphael created this painting of an Innu camp.

Food

Using birchbark canoes, snowshoes, toboggans, or sleds, the Innu travelled from place to place to hunt and gather food. They hunted caribou, moose, sea mammals, fish, and birds, and also gathered berries and roots. The Innu held special feasts to thank the animals for giving their lives. They knew that they depended on the animals to survive. When they killed an animal, they used every part of the animal out of respect.

The Innu were also able to trade for food with some First Nations peoples in the south. For example, the Innu obtained cornmeal from First Nations peoples who farmed. Cornmeal is a coarse flour made by grinding corn.

SPRING / SUMMER
- travelled to the coast to hunt sea mammals and to fish
- berries and moose or caribou meat were used to make pemmican for winter

WINTER / FALL
- moved inland to hunt caribou
- hunted ducks and geese

The Innu used their knowledge of the changing seasons and animal migration to travel and hunt.

Shelter

The Innu lived in temporary, cone-shaped wigwams. Usually, one or two families lived in each wigwam. These structures were easy to put up and take down. When the Innu moved, they left the frame behind but took the hides and bark with them.

Clothing

Innu women made clothing from the skins and furs of caribou and other animals. The caribou's fur trapped air and provided extra warmth during the cold northern winters. Innu women also made some clothing from sealskin, which was waterproof. They made moccasins from moose skin, which was thick and durable.

To build a wigwam, the Innu made a frame of wood poles and covered it with caribou hides and birchbark. What other natural items do you notice in this image?

Decision Making

The Innu usually lived in groups of several related families. An Elder who was the most respected hunter generally led the group. Although everyone took part in making decisions, the leader made the most important decisions, such as when to move camp. Sometimes, the situation they faced affected who would lead. For example, a person of great strength and strategy might be called on to lead in a time of war. A person skilled in tracking and in animal behaviour might be asked to lead a hunt.

Explore and Apply

1. What connections can you make to what you have learned about the Innu?
2. Create a graphic organizer to compare the ways of life of the Innu and the Wendat. Construct a map, locating both peoples, to support your comparison.

What Did First Nations Peoples Believe?

Spirituality

Elders taught that Earth and everything on Earth were made by the Creator or Great Spirit. The animals, plants, rocks, and water, as well as the Moon and Sun, all had a spirit and had to be respected. This understanding was an important part of First Nations peoples' beliefs.

First Nations peoples were thankful for the Creator's gifts. They were aware that their daily lives depended on these gifts. For example, the Wendat thought corn was such an important food that they held ceremonies to thank the Creator for it. Out of respect, Mi'kmaq hunters buried the bones of the moose that they hunted or used the bones to make items. The Mi'kmaq did not want to offend the spirits in any way, because if they did, they believed their next hunt would not be successful.

> **Faith in Action**
>
> Thunder Bay Catholic Schools are running an I Am Norm campaign to encourage respect, understanding, and acceptance. Students are actively involved in changing how they act toward each other. They are redefining the word *normal* and accepting one another.

Melissa Muir, Scott Sampson, and Darla Martens-Reece created this painting in 2007. It is called *Seven Sacred Grandfather Teachings*. Think about the words used in this painting. What connections can you make between these teachings and the Catholic Social Teachings?

The Anishinabe learned respect for Creation from the Seven Grandfather Teachings. The Seven Grandfathers were spirits who gave their teachings to a baby boy to pass on to all humans. These teachings were wisdom, love, respect, courage, honesty, humility, and truth. They guided the way that humans should act toward each other.

Sacred Objects

First Nations peoples used a variety of objects for spiritual ceremonies and celebrations. These objects included masks. In some First Nations communities, masks were worn by shamans in ceremonies to heal the sick. **Shamans** are spiritual leaders. They can be men or women. There are different kinds of shamans, such as those who heal the sick, predict the future, control the weather, or find lost objects.

Other sacred objects included drums, pipes, and dream catchers. All of these objects remain sacred today.

Catholic Connection

At the Anishinabe Spiritual Centre in Espanola, Ontario, young people can take workshops to learn about their spiritual lives. Jesuits and First Nations peoples run the centre together. The teachings of the centre are based on Catholic and First Nations beliefs.

This photo from 2009 shows Algonkin shaman Jacob Wawatie picking herbs in a forest near Kokomville, Québec.

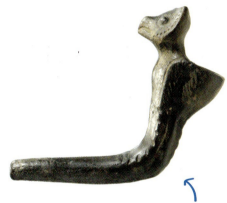

For special occasions, the Wendat used clay pipes decorated with animal images. Smoke from burning tobacco carried a person's thoughts and prayers to the Creator.

Explore and Apply

1. Why do you think the Anishinabe still follow the Seven Grandfather Teachings today?
2. Write a prayer connected to one of the Seven Grandfather Teachings.

Chapter 6 First Nations Peoples in Eastern Canada

Toolbox: Formulate Questions

Critical Questions

Remember, good critical questions help you identify, understand, and solve problems. They require you to dig deeper to interpret facts and information and analyze values and perspectives. You know your question is critical when it helps you make a reasoned judgment.

All research begins with questions. To formulate effective questions for your inquiry, follow these steps:

1. Think about the topic to determine your main ideas.

2. Use a graphic organizer to sort your main ideas.

3. Develop probing questions to focus your research. The information gained by answering these questions will lead to a deeper understanding of the topic.

4. As you gather information, stop to reflect on your questions. Decide if your questions need to change.

Nick wondered how First Nations peoples lived. He decided to compare the way of life of two First Nations. He developed a graphic organizer to record his ideas.

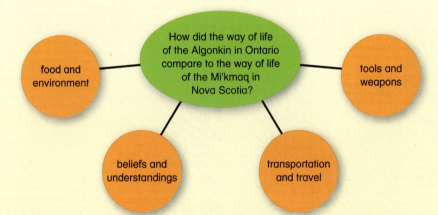

Nick had heard oral histories about the Algonkin in Ontario from his grandmother, and he had read stories about the Mi'kmaq in Nova Scotia. To find more specific information, Nick created some probing questions:

- How did the environment affect the way each group travelled?

- How were the beliefs of the Algonkin and Mi'kmaq the same? How were they different?

- What do the foods they ate reveal about their environment?

- What did both nations use to make tools and/or weapons?

- What do petroglyphs, or rock carvings, tell us about these two First Nations?

Nick decided to investigate petroglyphs.

> **Inquiry**
> Formulate Questions

Algonkin

The Algonkin and other First Nations peoples carved these petroglyphs. The carvings show people travelling by canoe and hunting. The human figure with the rays above his head is believed to be a shaman.

Petroglyphs Provincial Park, Ontario

Mi'kmaq

Many of the Mi'kmaq petroglyphs show an imaginary bird called the Kulloo. This bird represents the storytelling traditions of the Mi'kmaq. Storytelling was an important part of everyday life.

Petroglyphs in Kejimkujik National Park are considered a valuable artifact of the Mi'kmaq. Unfortunately, the petroglyphs are threatened by weather and vandalism. The park is trying to protect these artifacts for future generations.

Kejimkujik National Historic Site, Nova Scotia

Explore and Apply

1. What have you learned from examining the petroglyphs? What would you want to ask an Elder about these petroglyphs?
2. Create a graphic organizer to record the information that you have learned.

How Did First Nations Peoples Interact with Each Other?

Each nation lived in its own territory. However, nations also travelled great distances to meet one another. These meetings were a time to share ideas, renew friendships, and develop alliances. Some nations developed friendly relationships, while others had rivalries with each other.

> **Allies and Alliances**
>
> **Allies** are people or groups who work together for a common purpose. The word *alliance* comes from the word *ally* and means an agreement between two or more groups to work together and support each other.

This photo shows the Serpent Mounds (a sacred burial site) in Ohio, United States. These mounds are similar to ones near Peterborough, Ontario. This similarity suggests that early peoples shared, connected, and traded with peoples much farther away.

Trade

Many First Nations built relationships with other nations to trade for items that they could not find in their environment. They traded items such as food and tools. For example, the Wendat often had more corn than they needed. They traded for fish from the Nipissing, their northern neighbour.

Conflicts

At times, there were conflicts between neighbouring nations. The three main causes of conflict were

- disputes over hunting areas
- access to trade routes
- competition for trading partners

For example, the Wendat and Haudenosaunee sometimes were in conflict with each other because they produced the same types of goods (corn) and needed the same types of items (furs).

Alliances

Following years of conflict, some First Nations formed alliances. Alliances allowed them to keep the peace and continue trading. Some nations made alliances to support and protect each other during times of conflict.

Some First Nations peoples, such as the Wendat and Haudenosaunee, recorded important alliances on *wampum* belts. **Wampum** are beads made from shells that are strung together in patterns to make belts. White beads stood for peace and friendship. Purple beads represented conflict or an event of great importance. Wampum belts were worn for official purposes and in religious ceremonies.

Many First Nations peoples also used a pipe ceremony to mark an important alliance. Tobacco represented honesty. Smoking the peace pipe together meant that people would be truthful and respect the agreements made.

This photo shows Six Nations teacher Tom Deer demonstrating how to read a wampum belt. He uses artifacts like these to teach children in the Six Nations community about their history.

The Haudenosaunee Confederacy

The Haudenosaunee Confederacy was an alliance of five First Nations who joined together around 1100. Previously, the Mohawk, Seneca, Onondaga, Oneida, and Cayuga had been at war with each other. A Wendat man, who came to be known as the Great Peacemaker, called for peace. Hiawatha, an Onondaga man, and Jikonsaseh, a Seneca woman, helped to persuade the five nations to accept peace. The five nations agreed to unite and live under the Great Law of Peace. This became the nations' constitution and was based on values of peace, unity, and respect.

Did You Know?

The Haudenosaunee Confederacy is one of the oldest representative democracies in the world. **Representative democracy** is a form of government in which people elect leaders to represent their views and concerns. Canada is a representative democracy.

In 1722, the Tuscarora joined the Confederacy and these nations together became the Six Nations. After the nations joined together, each nation continued to keep its own culture and territory. Examine the map and consider why forming an alliance would have been essential for these First Nations peoples.

The Great Tree of Peace stands for unity for the Haudenosaunee. Its broad branches provide shelter. The eagle can see far and warn the nations of danger from enemies. The roots spread out, welcoming others to join. When the five nations planted the Great Tree of Peace, they threw their weapons beneath its roots, as a promise to end conflict.

To maintain this peace, the nations followed the teachings of the Peacemaker. They grouped themselves into clans. Several families of the same clan lived together in a longhouse. All of the people in the longhouse were related through their mother's family. The person in charge of the longhouse was the Clan Mother.

Men and women took part in making decisions for the clan. They gathered in separate councils and discussed issues and concerns, then shared their thoughts with the Clan Mother.

The Clan Mother chose a man in her clan to be chief and represent the clan at the Grand Council. The Grand Council was a gathering of chiefs from all longhouses in the five nations. It met to discuss matters that affected the entire Confederacy. Every chief had a chance to speak at the Grand Council. The Clan Mother attended the gatherings to ensure her chief was representing the views of the clan.

Thinking about Patterns and Trends

The Mi'kmaq were allies with other nearby nations. These nations eventually formed the seven-nation Wabanaki Confederacy. Think about what you have learned about other First Nations alliances and confederacies. Why do you think the Wabanaki Confederacy was formed?

How the Grand Council of Five Nations Made Decisions

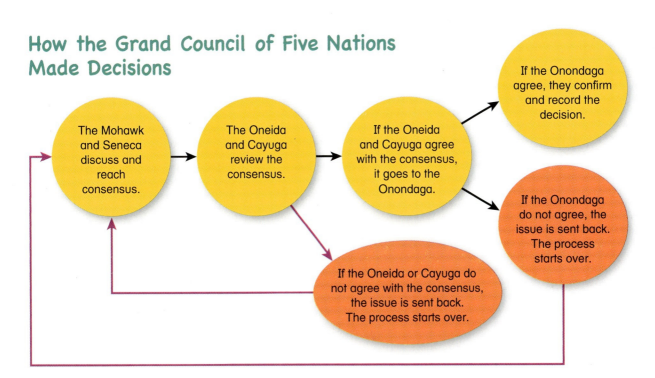

Explore and Apply

1. Why do you think the nations of the Haudenosaunee Confederacy were organized into clans? What benefits do clans provide?

2. Create a flow chart to show how decisions are made in your family or community.

Pulling It Together

How Can We Be Good Members of a Community?

Father Mike Explains...
Many First Nations communities show a spirit of solidarity. In Catholic teaching, solidarity is the firm determination to commit oneself to the common good because all of us are responsible for all.

See
What does Nick learn about First Nations communities long ago?

Reflect
Every person is the living image of God, so the good of each must be the concern of each. Explain what this means to you.

Act
Decide on one thing you can do with others to make life better for your class, family, or community. Do it.

First Nations peoples long ago had different ways of life, but they all belonged to communities. Even though communities were made up of different families, they lived like one big family. They worked together and took care of each other. Peace, unity, and respect were important.

My community may look different from that of my ancestors, but the way we live and work together is similar. We care for each other and for our community. I think peace, unity, and respect are still really important.

Nick

Belonging to a community also means taking part in its celebrations. Every year, members of the Six Nations hold festivals to celebrate their cultures.

Summarizing

Construct a map showing where the First Nations peoples were located in eastern Canada. Use the map to summarize your learning in this chapter. You can add words, phrases, symbols, or images to the map. You may also want to add questions to your map.

Making Connections

Add connections to the map you made for the Summarizing activity. Your connections can include
- text-to-self connections
- text-to-text connections
- text-to-world connections

Saint John XXIII said ...
 The family is the first essential cell of human society.

Chapter Inquiry

Choose one section in this chapter. Create a mind map to record the main ideas related to the topic in that section. List the questions you still have. Review your questions to check that they are digging deeper into the topic. Choose one critical question that you want to research further.

Chapter 7

Early Contact
1000–Early 1600s

Big Question

How did relationships between First Nations peoples and Europeans develop?

Learning Goals

- identify some early European explorers and their reasons for exploration
- gather and organize information from primary and secondary sources
- describe the impact of contact between European explorers and First Nations peoples

Hi, I'm Shamina.

I live in Corner Brook, Newfoundland and Labrador. Last weekend, I went camping with my Girl Guide group in Gros Morne National Park.

Our guide leader explained that we had the right to visit this beautiful park and use its resources, but we also had responsibilities. We had to take care of the land, clean up after ourselves, and respect others.

One of my tasks was to use a compass. It made me wonder about the first explorers who came to Canada. Why did they come? How did they find their way around in Canada?

Gros Morne National Park has been named a World Heritage Site because of its rich wildlife and unique rocks.

Our Faith

Saint John Paul II said ...

❝ The freedom of each human individual and community must respect the freedom and rights of other individuals and communities. ❞

134 Many Gifts Unit 2

Why Did European Explorers Sail to Canada?

The Vikings were probably the first Europeans to land in what is now Canada. They arrived in the year 1000, looking for places to live and people to trade with.

In the 1400s, other European explorers began sailing across the Atlantic Ocean. There were several reasons for these explorers to come to Canada. For a long time, Europeans had traded with India and China. However, the overland journey east through Europe and Asia was long and dangerous. European rulers wanted to find a water route to the west. In the search for this route, explorers came upon the land that would eventually become Canada.

Another reason for exploring was that the rulers of most European countries, including France and England, were competing with each other for wealth and power. They believed that one way to gain wealth and power was to own and control more land. Rulers sent people on expeditions to explore lands and claim them for their countries. Some of these lands became colonies.

Expedition and Colony

An **expedition** is a journey that is organized for a specific purpose. A **colony** is an area claimed and controlled by a country in another part of the world. Often, the newcomers displaced **indigenous** peoples (original people of the land).

This modern map of the world can help you understand where the explorers came from and where they went. Sweden, Norway, and Denmark are the modern countries where Vikings once lived. The United Kingdom includes England.

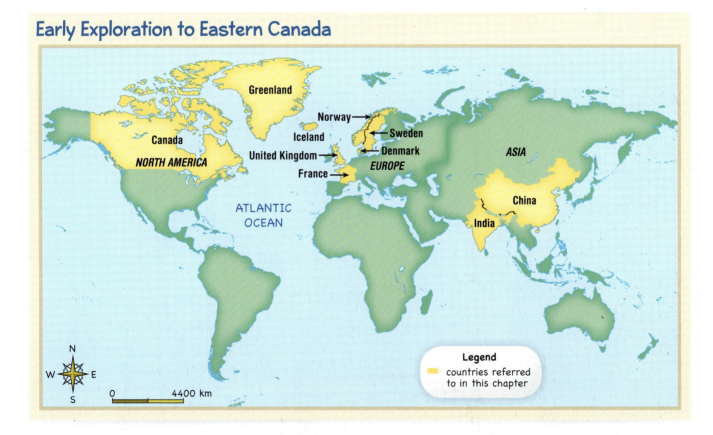

Early Exploration to Eastern Canada

Chapter 7 Early Contact

Reasons for Exploring

Trade Route to Asia
Many explorers were looking for a water route to Asia so they could trade for tea, spices, and silks.

Land and Power
Explorers claimed land on behalf of European rulers. Once the land was claimed, settlements developed.

Resources and Wealth
Many explorers wanted to obtain gold, silver, timber, furs, fish, and other resources.

Religion
European Christians wanted to spread their faith to people in other lands.

Curiosity and Adventure
Some early European explorers were curious about the adventures and riches that could be found across the Atlantic Ocean.

Sailing Ships and Navigation

At this time, many parts of the world were unmapped. If there were maps, they were often incomplete or incorrect. People did not have the kinds of technology that we have today to travel and help them find their way. Sailors looked at the positions of the Sun and the stars to help them determine where they were. They used their knowledge of the sea to help them navigate through uncharted waters. For example, when sailors saw shorebirds, they knew that land was approaching.

In the 1400s, Europeans built ships that moved faster than ships had previously. They also improved navigation tools, such as the compass and astrolabe. These tools helped explorers find their way and travel farther than they had before.

Catholic Connection

For thousands of years, people have looked to the stars to help them find their way. The Christmas story in the Bible tells of the journey of the Three Wise Men following a star to find the baby Jesus.

By pointing astrolabes like this one at the Sun or the North Star, explorers were able to locate their positions at sea.

During the time of early European explorers, people thought that if they travelled west from Europe, they would arrive in Asia. This map shows their thinking. Spain is in the top right corner, and India is on the far left. This map has been reconstructed from a map created in 1474 by Italian mathematician Paolo dal Pozzo Toscanelli.

Here and Now

People continue to explore. They explore other planets, such as Mars, and they explore the depths of the oceans.

Explore and Apply

1. Would you want to be an explorer? Why, or why not?
2. Construct a map to show what you have learned so far about early explorers. Add to the map as you continue learning throughout this chapter.

Spotlight on the Norse

Who Were the Norse?

Over 1000 years ago, some of the Norse left their homelands and sailed west across the Atlantic Ocean. Along the way, they colonized different places, including Iceland and Greenland. Norse explorers were called Vikings.

Sagas are long stories that tell about heroes, especially those of the Norse. Some Norse sagas tell of a sailor named Bjarni Herjólfsson. While sailing from Iceland to Greenland around the year 985, his ship was blown off course. After many days of sailing through fog, he sailed past what was probably the coast of Labrador and headed back to Greenland.

Herjólfsson told stories of what he had seen. Around the year 1000, another Viking named Leif Eriksson decided to set off to these lands. One saga describes how Eriksson explored parts of northern and eastern Canada. Many historians believe that Eriksson and his crew were the first Europeans to set foot in North America.

Did You Know?
Thjodhild Jorundardaughter, mother of Leif Eriksson, established the first Christian church in Greenland, according to a Norse saga.

Today, we call the site where the Vikings built a settlement L'Anse aux Meadows.

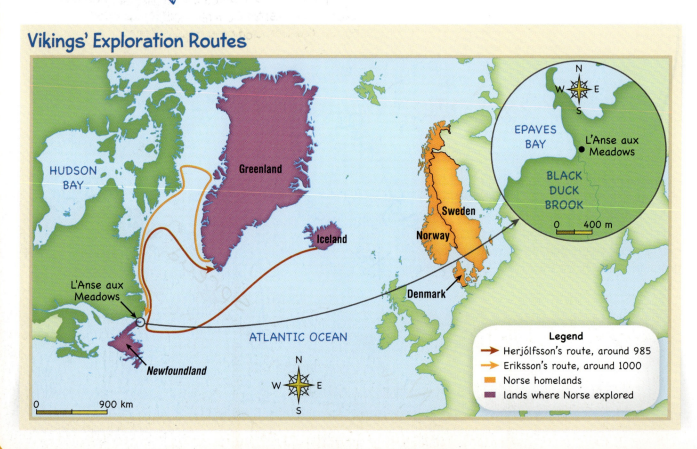

Vikings' Exploration Routes

Legend
- Herjólfsson's route, around 985
- Eriksson's route, around 1000
- Norse homelands
- lands where Norse explored

What Is L'Anse aux Meadows?

L'Anse aux Meadows was the very first European settlement in North America. Archaeologists think that this settlement was a place where the Norse stayed in winter to repair their boats and prepare for their journeys back to Greenland.

Norse sagas tell that the Vikings traded with First Nations peoples, probably the Beothuk, Innu, and Mi'kmaq. First Nations peoples provided the Vikings with furs in exchange for iron goods. Many encounters between the Norse and First Nations peoples ended in conflict.

After some years, the Norse loaded their ships with wood and furs and returned to Greenland. No one knows for certain why the Norse left.

First Nations at L'Anse aux Meadows

First Nations peoples had lived at the site of L'Anse aux Meadows long before the Norse arrived. Aboriginal artifacts found there date back about 6000 years.

When the Vikings arrived on Canada's coast, they saw abundant forests, as well as streams full of fish. Since the Viking ships were made of wood, this land provided them with a much-needed supply of lumber. This photo shows a replica of a Viking ship. Replicas like this are created from historical sources and information collected by archaeologists.

How Was L'Anse aux Meadows Uncovered?

For hundreds of years, the settlement at L'Anse aux Meadows lay in ruins. The ruins became overgrown.

In 1960, explorer Helge Ingstad and archaeologist Anne Stine Ingstad travelled from Norway to the island of Newfoundland. Helge Ingstad had studied the Vikings and read their sagas. He wanted to look for evidence of a settlement. A local resident told him of some strange mounds and ridges in the ground to the north. After Helge Ingstad found the site, Anne Stine Ingstad supervised the excavation.

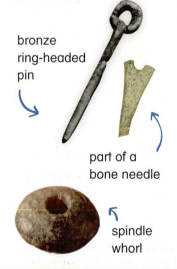

These are a few of the artifacts found at L'Anse aux Meadows. The discovery of the bone needle and spindle whorl has led archaeologists to believe that Norse women lived in this settlement.

bronze ring-headed pin

part of a bone needle

spindle whorl

Helge Ingstad uncovers a stone fireplace.

Anne Stine Ingstad works at the archaeological site.

Over the next eight years, archaeologists from around the world worked on the site and uncovered the remains of buildings. The buildings had a similar structure and design to those in Iceland and Greenland from the same period.

Inside the structures, archaeologists found a number of items confirming that this was an early Viking settlement. They found a bronze ring-headed pin, which is a type of clasp that the Norse wore on their cloaks. They also found a piece of a bone needle and a small spindle whorl, which is part of a tool used for spinning fibres into thread.

What Was the Settlement Like?

The settlement at L'Anse aux Meadows has been reconstructed using archaeologists' findings.

This photo shows the outside of the reconstructed buildings.

Thinking about Significance

People from all over the world visit L'Anse aux Meadows to see what it was like, and to learn about the Vikings. Many people consider the site a significant part of Canadian history. What do you think makes it significant?

This photo shows the inside of the reconstructed dwelling. Viking dwellings housed many families. A variety of activities occurred within, including carpentry and weaving.

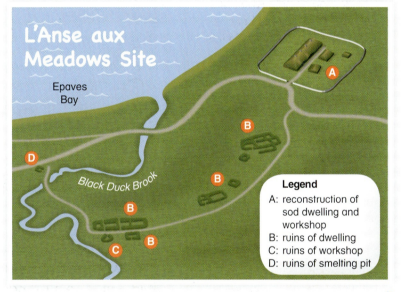

This diagram shows the buildings that were found at L'Anse aux Meadows. Iron from nearby was processed in the smelting pit. The iron was then made into tools in a room in one of the dwellings. What can you tell about what life might have been like back then?

Explore and Apply

1. Do you think it is important to reconstruct the ruins of ancient buildings? Why, or why not?

2. The museum curators at L'Anse aux Meadows have asked you to create a poster to promote tourism. What aspects of life at L'Anse aux Meadows will you highlight?

Who Were Some of the Other Early European Explorers?

Oral stories of some eastern First Nations peoples tell about the arrival of fair-skinned strangers. A Mi'kmaq story tells how a girl dreamed that she saw a floating island. On the island were trees and living creatures. A day later, her dream came true as an island floated toward shore. The island turned out to be a ship carrying Europeans. This was the Mi'kmaq's first meeting with Europeans.

Explorers of Eastern Canada

The earliest Europeans to arrive in eastern Canada thought they had reached India. They quickly realized their mistake. They also realized that First Nations peoples were already living there, and that this land was rich in resources. Soon, many European explorers came seeking wealth.

John Cabot

In the late 1400s, the king of England hired Italian explorer Giovanni Caboto to look for a water route to Asia. This explorer is known as John Cabot in English. Cabot landed on what is believed to be Canada's east coast and claimed it for England. He named the land that he saw "New Found Land."

When Cabot returned to England, he told about waters that were full of fish. News spread. European fishers began travelling to the waters off the island of Newfoundland to fish.

> **Catholic Connection**
>
> During the 1400s, many Europeans were Christian and did not eat meat on certain days. Instead, they ate fish. This tradition of eating fish on certain days continues today.

John Cabot

COUNTRY: England

EXPLORATION FACTS: Cabot made two journeys, in 1497 and 1498. His second journey remains clouded in mystery. Historians believe Cabot and his crew were lost at sea.

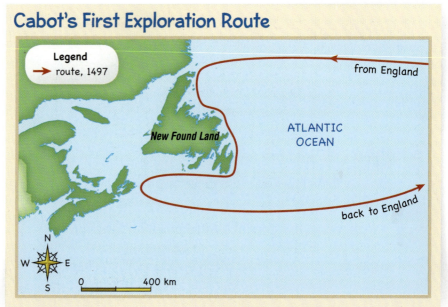

Cabot's First Exploration Route

Legend: route, 1497

Jacques Cartier

The king of France heard stories about the successful explorations of other European countries. In 1534, he chose Jacques Cartier to explore and claim lands for France, and to find a water route to Asia.

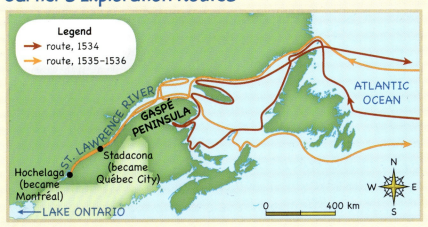

Cartier's Exploration Routes

Jacques Cartier

COUNTRY: France

EXPLORATION FACTS: Cartier made two journeys to explore the east coast, the first in 1534, the second starting in 1535. In 1541, Cartier returned to Canada, leading 1500 French colonists to settle near Stadacona. The settlement lasted less than a year.

Samuel de Champlain

In 1603, the French sent an expedition to Nova Scotia and Québec. A mapmaker named Samuel de Champlain was part of this expedition. Champlain would later go on to explore and map areas farther west.

A 16-year-old boy named Étienne Brûlé travelled with Champlain to Canada. Brûlé went on many expeditions for Champlain to explore farther inland.

Champlain's and Brûlé's Exploration Routes

Samuel de Champlain

COUNTRY: France

EXPLORATION FACTS: Between 1609 and 1616, Champlain spent many months exploring the St. Lawrence River and Great Lakes area. He was greatly aided by First Nations guides.

Chapter 7 Early Contact

Explorers of Northeastern Canada

Like the Mi'kmaq, Inuit also have stories about how their ancestors met foreigners. Their stories tell of tall, blond men in "funny boats" sailing by their shores. The first of these explorers might have been the Vikings.

Martin Frobisher and Henry Hudson

Two of the earliest Europeans to explore Canada's northeast were Martin Frobisher and Henry Hudson. Both explorers were looking for a northern route through the Arctic islands to Asia.

Martin Frobisher

COUNTRY: England

EXPLORATION FACTS: Frobisher made three voyages, in 1576, 1577, and 1578. In 1578, he filled 15 ships with a shiny mineral he thought was gold. It was not gold, but iron pyrite, or fool's gold.

Frobisher's and Hudson's Exploration Routes

Legend
- Frobisher's route, 1577
- Hudson's route, 1610–1611

Martin Frobisher named a bay after himself when he came upon it, thinking the bay led to Asia. Later, English colonists named Hudson Bay after Henry Hudson.

Henry Hudson

COUNTRY: England

EXPLORATION FACTS: Hudson made one journey to explore this area, starting in 1610. It ended in mutiny in 1611. Hudson's crew abandoned him on the coast of what would become James Bay.

Explore and Apply

1. What connections can you make between exploration in the past and exploration today?
2. Create an exploration timeline. Indicate the country that each explorer represented.

What Were Some Benefits of Contact?

When French and English explorers landed in Canada, they soon met First Nations peoples. Many of these meetings were friendly and benefited both sides.

First Nations peoples often welcomed the explorers with kindness. In 1535, when Cartier visited the village of Hochelaga (at the site of present-day Montréal), the people there greeted him warmly. They offered him fish and other gifts of food.

Thinking about Cause and Consequence

In 1694, Sadakanahtie, an Onondaga chief, described how First Nations peoples welcomed the explorers. He said that the First Nations peoples tied the explorer's large sailing ships "not with a Rope made of Bark" but with a "strong iron Chain fastened to a great Mountain." Create a graphic organizer to show the causes and consequences of European explorers arriving in Canada. Add to your graphic organizer as you continue reading.

Andrew Morris created this artwork in 1850. It shows Cartier's first meeting with the people living in Hochelaga. Whose viewpoint is represented in this painting?

Exchanging Goods

Not long after First Nations peoples and Europeans met, they began to trade with each other. Both First Nations peoples and Europeans saw the benefit of trading. First Nations peoples traded for metal goods such as knives, axes, needles, weapons, and cooking pots. These metal products were stronger than the items made from stone or wood that First Nations peoples were using. In return, Europeans acquired beaver pelts, or furs. Pelts were very valuable in Europe for making clothing.

Sharing Knowledge

Early explorers relied on the knowledge and skills of First Nations peoples to help them find their way around and to survive on the land.

Geographical Knowledge

First Nations peoples shared their knowledge of water and land routes into the interior of Canada. For example, Brûlé lived with the Wendat for many years in the early 1600s. The Wendat shared with Brûlé their knowledge of the land. This allowed Brûlé to explore farther inland.

Faith in Action

Grades 4 and 5 students at St. Robert Catholic School in Toronto, Ontario, took part in an email exchange program with students in New Zealand. Students in both countries benefited from learning about each other's culture and country. Exchanging letters gave students the opportunity to share knowledge and show their respect for their different perspectives and cultural traditions.

This painting shows First Nations guides taking Champlain to Georgian Bay. In 1925, Charles William Jefferys created this painting, called *Champlain Discovers Georgian Bay*. How do you think First Nations peoples might respond to the title of this painting?

Here and Now

First Nations peoples invented items that we still use today, such as toboggans and snowshoes. As well, some ingredients we use in medicines today were first discovered by First Nations peoples. These include wild ginger, bloodroot, and seneca root.

Technologies

First Nations peoples helped European explorers to navigate in small, lightweight canoes. The large European ships could not travel up narrow streams and rivers. They also taught the explorers how to make snowshoes and toboggans. This helped the explorers to travel more efficiently across the snow.

Food and Medicine

First Nations peoples taught European explorers how to survive on the land. Explorers learned about native animals, plants, berries, and roots. For example, they learned that black cherry could be used as a remedy for coughs and colds.

In the winter of 1535, Cartier and his crew decided to stay at Stadacona, a First Nations village at the present-day site of Québec City. They had stayed in this village before. Unprepared for the cold, Cartier and his men suffered greatly. Their diet lacked fresh fruits and vegetables. Many of Cartier's crew became sick from an illness called scurvy. Some men even died. The people of Stadacona saved the lives of the remaining crew. They showed the French how to make a special tea from the bark and needles of white cedar trees. Each day, they also brought fresh fish and venison (deer meat) to help the French get well.

Did You Know?

Fruits and vegetables give your body a very important nutrient—vitamin C. Many early explorers and sailors lacked vitamin C. Without vitamin C, they suffered from scurvy. The effects of scurvy include fever, loose teeth, swollen arms and legs, and even death.

This painting was created in 1928 by Hal Ross Perrigard. It is called *The Virtue of the Tree Annedda*. The needles of the annedda (a coniferous tree) were used to make a cure for scurvy. Whose viewpoint is represented in this painting?

Explore and Apply

1. Which piece of knowledge that First Nations peoples shared with Europeans do you consider most important? Why?

2. Through trade, First Nations peoples obtained metal goods. What impact do you think these goods had on the lives of First Nations peoples? Support your answer.

3. Create a graphic organizer showing the advantages of contact between First Nations peoples and Europeans. What conclusions can you draw?

What Conflicts Arose from Contact?

Contact between First Nations peoples and Europeans brought together very different cultures with very different views. These differences often led to conflict.

Different Views of the Land

First Nations peoples saw, and still see, themselves as part of the land. The land is not something that anyone owns or has control over. In the quotation below, Elder Twylah Hurd Nitsch of the Seneca First Nation describes her people's view of the land.

> ❝ Native people did not feel ownership of land or homes; they felt the responsibility of preserving [land] through caring for it. They maintained the area for future use and productivity. Land was a shared, living entity. ❞

European explorers viewed the land as property, something that could be bought or sold. Europe had a system of land ownership. Governments controlled the land and armies defended it. However, as far as the Europeans were concerned, First Nations peoples had no rights to the land. Explorers claimed the land for their king or queen.

Colonizing the World

French and English rulers were not just sending explorers to Canada. Explorers were also travelling to and claiming lands in South America, the Caribbean, Africa, and Australia. Indigenous peoples in these lands were often displaced as a result.

Other European countries, including Portugal and Spain, were also colonizing other continents around the globe. This often led to conflict between European countries.

This diagram represents the way many First Nations peoples viewed nature. They saw themselves as part of nature and connected to it.

This diagram represents the way Europeans viewed nature. They believed that humans were most important and that they had control over nature. Does either of these two diagrams represent your own view? Why or why not?

This difference in views toward the land could clearly be seen when Cabot reached the island of Newfoundland in 1497. Upon landing, he raised a cross and banner. This was a sign to other European countries that the land had been claimed and now belonged to the king of England. Cabot had spotted a used fire pit and a painted, carved stick, so he knew people already lived there. Still, he claimed the land for England.

In 1534, Cartier arrived in what is now Québec. He claimed the land for France by putting up a cross. A group of First Nations peoples and their leader, Chief Donnacona, had paddled up the St. Lawrence River from their village of Stadacona on a fishing trip. They watched Cartier and his men raise the cross and claim the land for France. Donnacona protested, but Cartier said that the cross was just a landmark to help him find his way back.

In 1938, John David Kelly created this painting of Cabot landing in what is now Canada. How do you think First Nations peoples living in this area might have responded to Cabot's actions?

Taken to Foreign Lands

European explorers often took First Nations peoples back to Europe with them. They hoped that First Nations peoples would learn the European language and be useful as translators and guides back in North America. As a result, many First Nations peoples died from European diseases.

On his first voyage, in 1534, Cartier wanted to prove to the king of France that he had claimed new lands for France. He convinced Chief Donnacona to let him take two young men in exchange for a hatchet and two knives. Donnacona viewed this exchange as a way to build trust and friendship. Cartier left for France, promising to return the following year. While in Europe, the two young men learned to speak French. Upon their return in 1535, they guided Cartier up the St. Lawrence River to their village in Stadacona.

> **Did You Know?**
> In 1542, Cartier sailed back to France. He took along some shiny rocks, thinking that they contained diamonds and gold. They turned out to be fool's gold.

In 1536, when Cartier returned to France, he took Donnacona and several others from the village. This time, all those he took died from European diseases, except for a little girl.

In 1541, Cartier sailed back to Québec without any of the villagers. The people of Stadacona were angered by this and no longer trusted him.

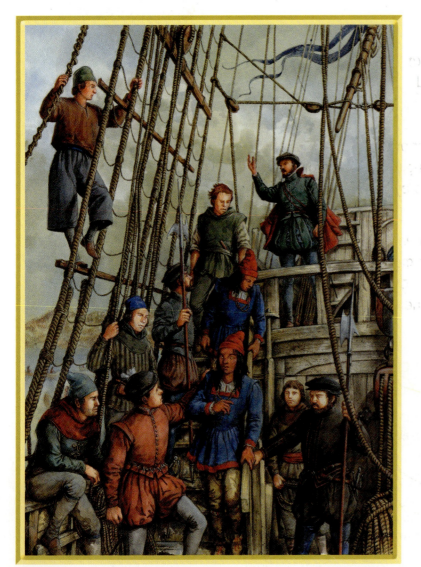

This painting by Francis Black shows the two men Cartier took back with him to France in 1534. How do you think the two men might have felt? Support your answer.

Communication

An inability to communicate sometimes resulted in conflict. In 1576, Inuit and the English came into contact when Frobisher sailed into the area around Baffin Island.

As the two groups communicated through hand gestures, Frobisher thought that Inuit were offering to guide him through the Arctic islands. He sent five of his crew ashore with a guide. The crew were never seen again. Frobisher searched, but could not find them. As revenge, he captured an Inuk man and took him back to England.

In 1577, Frobisher returned to Baffin Island. He found European clothes in an abandoned Inuit camp. He thought that these were from his missing crew and that Inuit had harmed them. In revenge, Frobisher attacked a nearby Inuit camp. Inuit were chased to the edge of the shore and fought back with arrows. According to an Inuit story, Inuit thought they were being attacked by beings from another world.

What did happen to Frobisher's five men? No one knows. An Inuit story tells that the men lived among them for a few years and were looked after. One day, the men sailed away in a boat that they built. No one saw them again.

John White painted this scene of the fight between Inuit and Frobisher's crew. Some historical accounts suggest that White may have travelled with Frobisher on his voyage in 1577. How might this painting be different if it were created from an Inuit perspective?

Explore and Apply

1. How did different views about the land lead to conflict between First Nations peoples and European explorers?

2. Choose one of the following scenes: Cartier raising the cross, First Nations peoples arriving in France, or the people of Stadacona seeing Cartier's ships return in 1541. With a group, role-play the discussion that might have taken place.

Faith in Action

Grades 4 to 6 students at the Toronto Catholic District School Board take part in a yearly event called the Northern Spirit Games. Students play traditional games to help them understand Aboriginal cultures.

Toolbox: Gather and Organize Information

Perspective

Perspective is the way people see the world. Perspective develops from a person's background knowledge, experiences, and values. When using primary and secondary sources, remember that each source presents the creator's perspective. Ask yourself the following:

- Who created this text or image? Why?
- What did this person value or believe?
- What or who was left out?

Gathering Information

1. Consider your inquiry question. Think about what you already know and what you want to find out.

2. Think about key words that can help you find useful information. Your sources can include books, magazines, interviews, documentaries, historical sites, museums, and the Internet.

3. Gather a variety of primary and secondary sources. Look for information from more than one perspective.

Internet Search Tips

- Read the "about the author" for the website, if there is one.
- Look for contact information to find out who published the resource.
- Identify the purpose of the website.

Shamina wants to research the inquiry question: How did both First Nations peoples and European explorers view the arrival of Europeans? She gathered information from library books, the Canadian Encyclopedia website, and other websites.

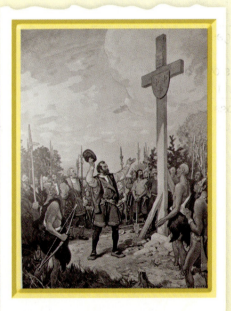

Charles William Jefferys created this artwork in 1925. It's called *Jacques Cartier Erects a Cross at Gaspé*. I wonder why the cross is so large.

The Mi'kmaq have an oral story that tells about the dream of a young Mi'kmaq girl. Before Jacques Cartier arrived in Canada, she dreamt about an island that was floating on the ocean. It drew closer toward land and she could see that there were many people and trees without branches on the island. The people wore strange white clothing.

***

When she awoke, she told the wise men all about her dream. They could not interpret her dream.

***

The oral story continues to explain that the next day, the Mi'kmaq saw an island floating toward the shore. It looked like there were trees on the island. Bears were climbing the trees. The Mi'kmaq grabbed their bows and arrows! Before they could shoot the bears, they realized the bears were really men. They had never seen such strange men before.

Inquiry
Gather and Organize Information

> " And pointing to the cross [the chief] made us a long [speech], making the sign of the cross with two of his fingers and then he pointed to the land all around about, as if he wished to say that all this region belonged to him, and that we ought not to have set up this cross without his permission. "

This quotation comes from Cartier's journal, but it was translated by H.P. Biggar in 1924 in his book *The Voyages of Jacques Cartier*. Cartier is describing Chief Donnacona's reaction to the cross Cartier used to claim the land.

Organizing Information

Organizing the information you find can help you identify whether you have enough. It can also help you begin to analyze it. There are different ways to organize information.

Shamina used this chart to help her consider the perspective in each source.

	Oral Story	Painting	Journal Entry
Source	website, no source provided	The artwork was created in 1925.	
Perspective	The oral story of a young Mi'kmaq girl.	The painter shows the event through the eyes of Cartier.	
What did I observe?	The Mi'kmaq were amazed when Europeans first came. They had never before seen boats like that.	Cartier is the largest person in the painting. The cross towers over all the men. No women are in the painting.	
What questions do I still have?	Are there other sources to back up this source? How do we know about an oral story from so long ago?	Why was the cross so big? Why didn't they use a flag?	

Once you have organized your information, reflect on what you have learned and what you still need to find out. Ask yourself: Do I have enough sources to give me different perspectives?

Explore and Apply

1. Does Shamina have enough reliable information to complete her inquiry successfully? Should she revise her question? Explain.
2. Complete the chart Shamina started, adding information about the journal entry.

Pulling It Together

Father Mike Explains ...

In the 1500s, most Europeans did not think First Nations peoples had rights. However, Father Francis of Vitoria (1483–1546) and Bishop Bartolome de Las Casas (1484–1566) insisted that *all* people have basic human rights. This is the official position of our Church.

See

What harm and what good did European explorers do?

Reflect

Why do you think explorers tended to cause harm to First Nations peoples they encountered?

Act

Brainstorm three ideas for repairing the harm that is done when people do not respect the rights of others.

Why Should We Respect the Dignity of Each Person?

Early European explorers believed that they had the right to explore and claim this land for their king or queen. They didn't respect the rights of First Nations peoples. Jesus taught us to love our neighbours as we do ourselves. I think that means it's important to respect people and their rights.

I learned that if First Nations peoples had not helped the explorers, it would have been very difficult for Europeans to survive. When I see new students or people new to Canada, I try to be friendly and help them out.

Shamina

This image shows thousands of people walking through Vancouver, British Columbia, on September 22, 2013, to show their belief in First Nations culture, nationhood, and justice.

Summarizing

Reflect on the most important ideas from this chapter. Complete the following sentence starters for one individual from this chapter:

This person did ...

This person wanted ...

This person interacted with (either in cooperation or in conflict) ...

As a result, this happened ...

Exchange your sentence with a partner to see if he or she can figure out who the person was.

Making Connections

Chris Hadfield is a Canadian astronaut. What challenges do you think he faced on his voyages? How were his challenges different from those of the European explorers? Consider which is more challenging: heading off across an unmapped ocean in a wooden boat 600 years ago or rocketing off into outer space today. Explain your reasoning.

Saint John Paul II said ...

> The freedom of each human individual and community must respect the freedom and rights of other individuals and communities.

Chapter Inquiry

After reading this chapter, what question(s) do you still have about European explorers? Use this chapter and other sources to gather information to answer one of your questions.

You may want to talk with other classmates and your teacher about the question. Are there experts you can speak with?

Look for information that provides more than one perspective on the topic. Find at least three sources of information.

Organize your information. Ask yourself: Do I have enough information? What else do I need to find? What questions do I still have?

Chapter 8

Fur Trade in Eastern Canada
1500s–1713

Big Question

How did the early fur trade affect the relationship between First Nations peoples and Europeans?

Learning Goals

- describe aspects of the interactions between First Nations and Europeans
- interpret and analyze information
- identify the consequences of the early fur trade

This photo shows a trading post in 1937. A father is trading the fur of a wolverine for food. The fur trade was still important hundreds of years after it first began.

Hi, I'm Aran.

I live in Thunder Bay, Ontario. In school, we're learning about the fur trade. I visited Fort William Historical Park with my family. It's a reconstruction of a trading post. A guide took us out in a canoe, just like fur traders long ago.

I wonder what fur trading was like. Did it help the lives of First Nations peoples? Was it fair?

Our Faith

Pope Paul VI said …

"Freedom of trade is fair only if it is subject to the demands of social justice."

On the Development of Peoples (no. 59)

How Did the Fur Trade Start?

Long before the arrival of Europeans, First Nations peoples had been trading furs, food, and other items with each other. They travelled long distances over land and water to trade.

In 1497, John Cabot returned to England after exploring the east coast of Canada. He told the English about the great supply of cod off the island of Newfoundland. Soon, the English and other Europeans began sailing to the shores of Newfoundland to fish. When they went ashore to dry their fish, they met the Beothuk, Mi'kmaq, and Wolastoqiyik. These First Nations peoples exchanged the furs they had trapped for iron goods that the fishers had brought with them.

This artwork was created around 1628 by an unknown European artist. It shows Beothuk people trading with the English in 1612. Some of the details in the artwork are inaccurate. For example, the Beothuk did not use the type of canoe shown. Why might inaccuracies occur when artists base their work on first-hand accounts?

The Beothuk people no longer exist. They disappeared as a result of European diseases and conflict. Most of what we know about the Beothuk comes from the stories and drawings of Shanawdithit (shown here). She was the last of the Beothuk people. She died in 1829.

> **"** They held up some furs of small value, with which they clothe themselves. We likewise made signs to them that we wished them no harm, and sent two men on shore, to offer them some knives and other iron goods, and a red cap to give to their chief. **"**

Jacques Cartier wrote in his journal about exchanging iron goods for furs with the Mi'kmaq.

Chapter 8 Fur Trade in Eastern Canada

Fashion and the Demand for Fur

In the 1600s, there was a growing demand for fur in Europe. Clothing made with fur was a sign of wealth and power. This made fur very valuable. Hats made from beaver fur were the most popular. Beaver fur was soft, smooth, waterproof, and long-lasting. However, because of over-hunting, there were almost no beavers left in Europe.

French and English merchants sent fur traders to Canada to get beaver furs. **Merchants** are people who buy and sell goods. European fur traders were unfamiliar with the Canadian land, so they turned to First Nations peoples for help.

France and England both competed for furs in Canada. This competition changed trading relations between First Nations and Europeans. Trade shifted from the friendly exchange of goods between individuals to a competitive business between nations.

Demand for beaver fur continued in Europe for a few hundred years. These are examples of beaver hats from the 1700s to the 1800s. Other furs, such as fox and wolf, were also valuable.

"CONTINENTAL" HAT

NAVAL COCKED HAT

A CLERICAL TYPE

ARMY HAT

THE PARIS BEAU

THE WELLINGTON

THE D'ORSAY

THE REGENT

Explore and Apply

1. In your own words, explain what happened as a result of the growing demand for beaver fur in Europe.

2. Create an ad for fur hats that might have appeared in an early European magazine. Include a slogan, a description, and an illustration.

How Was Trade Conducted?

For First Nations peoples, meetings for trade were social events. Trading provided an opportunity to share gifts, news, and ideas. For Europeans, trade was simply a matter of business and a way to make money.

Europeans built trading posts along waterways. First Nations peoples came to these posts in canoes filled with furs. They exchanged furs for European goods, such as kettles, pots, scissors, fishing hooks, and blankets. Trading goods for goods, without the use of money, is called **bartering**.

Over time, Europeans established specific values for different items.

Catholic Connection

The Bible says, "When you make a sale to your neighbour or buy from your neighbour, you shall not cheat one another." (Leviticus 25:14, NRSV)

Sample Values from 1706

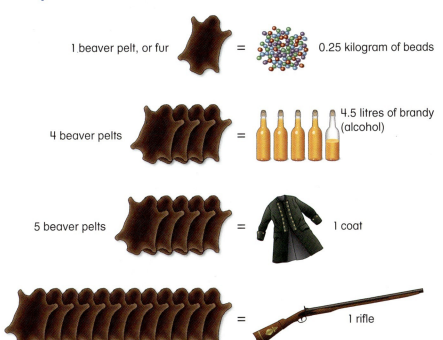

1 beaver pelt, or fur = 0.25 kilogram of beads

4 beaver pelts = 4.5 litres of brandy (alcohol)

5 beaver pelts = 1 coat

12 beaver pelts = 1 rifle

Faith in Action

In 2012, students at O'Gorman Intermediate Catholic School in Timmins, Ontario, hosted the Ten Thousand Villages International Gift Festival to raise awareness of fair trade. At the event, students sold crafts made by skilled workers in developing countries. The money raised was sent to the workers.

Explore and Apply

1. List some of the advantages and disadvantages of bartering for goods, rather than using money.

2. Begin a graphic organizer to show the causes and consequences of the fur trade for both First Nations peoples and Europeans. Add to this graphic organizer as you read through the chapter.

Chapter 8 Fur Trade in Eastern Canada

What Were the Roles of First Nations Men and Women in the Fur Trade?

First Nations men studied the habits of the beaver. They trapped the animals during winter, when the fur was thickest. In spring, they paddled to fur-trading posts to barter with European fur traders.

As well, First Nations men used established trading networks to expand the fur trade. Some worked as go-betweens. That meant they traded for furs from First Nations trappers who lived farther inland. For example, the Wendat bartered for furs from the Nipissing, a people who lived near what is now Sudbury. The Wendat then brought the furs south to French trading posts along the St. Lawrence River.

European fur traders depended on First Nations men as guides. The guides showed them the best land trails and water routes.

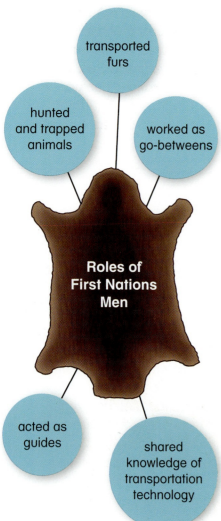

Roles of First Nations Men:
- transported furs
- hunted and trapped animals
- worked as go-betweens
- acted as guides
- shared knowledge of transportation technology

First Nations peoples taught fur traders how to build canoes, snowshoes, and sleds. These transportation methods made it much easier to move furs and other goods through the woods and along rivers and streams. This photo shows an exhibit from the Canadian Canoe Museum in Peterborough, Ontario. This museum preserves canoes, teaches visitors about the history of canoes, and celebrates our fur-trading past.

First Nations women prepared the furs for transportation to Europe. They cleaned, scraped, stretched, and dried the skins. First Nations women also worked alongside men to build and repair canoes.

First Nations women helped the European fur traders in their daily lives. They provided the fur traders with much of the food that they needed. They also made clothing for the fur traders that was suitable for the colder climate. First Nations women also shared their knowledge of different plants for making medicines.

Many First Nations women married European fur traders. The women learned their husband's language and culture. Many women acted as guides and interpreters. They helped build good relations between cultures. Their children learned skills from both parents.

Did You Know?

European traders preferred fur that was old, since it was softer. Some First Nations peoples were surprised that Europeans were willing to exchange valuable metal items for what they saw as old clothing.

First Nations peoples also traded the hides of moose, caribou, and other animals with Europeans. These hides were used to make leather products, such as gloves and vests. This artwork by Charles William Jefferys shows a First Nations woman preparing moose hide.

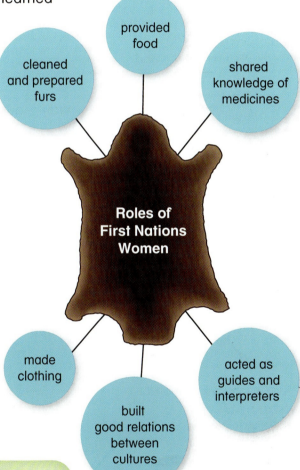

Explore and Apply

1. How was the fur trade an exchange of both goods and ideas?
2. With a small group, develop and perform a dialogue in role. Show how First Nations peoples helped early European fur traders.

Toolbox: Interpret and Analyze Information

Interpret and Analyze

When you interpret, you explain or restate information in your own words to help you understand it. You might use sentences that start with "Another way of saying that is ..." or "The text is suggesting that ..."

When you analyze, you dig deeper to get to the heart of the matter. You take something apart to find out how it works. You ask probing questions to build a deeper understanding.

Interpreting and Analyzing Text

1. Look for the main points or ideas in each piece of information. Is the information on topic? Is supporting evidence provided?

2. Decide if you have enough information to answer your inquiry question. Is anything missing? Continue your research to fill in any gaps that you see.

3. Identify any patterns and connections among all the pieces of information. Look for the following:
   - similarities and differences
   - causes and consequences
   - new information and information you have seen before

4. Reflect on any new understandings that you have gained based on the patterns and connections.

Aran gathered the following information about the fur trade to help him answer his inquiry question: How did different people view the fur trade?

An Innu chief said to a French Jesuit priest, Father Paul Le Jeune, "The beaver does everything perfectly well; it makes kettles, hatchets, swords, knives, bread; and in short, it makes everything. The English have no sense, they give us twenty knives like this for one beaver skin."

—*Jesuit Relations*, 1610–1791

We [the English] started a fur trade company whose main purpose was "for the Discovery of a new Passage into [Asia] and for the finding [of] some Trade for Furs, Minerals, and other [valuable products]."

—*The Royal Charter for Incorporating the Hudson's Bay Company*, 1670

This painting was created in 1921 by an unknown artist. It is called *Ceremony of the Pipe*.

For First Nations, exchanging goods was an act of respect and goodwill. Trade meetings were a chance to make new friends and strengthen relationships.

Inquiry
Interpret and Analyze

Interpreting and Analyzing Images

1. Look at the details in any images you have found.
   - Who is in the image? What are they doing?
   - Whose perspective is the image showing? How do you know?

2. Notice the body language and the facial expressions of any people in the image.
   - What is the artist showing about how people feel?
   - What is the artist suggesting about how people are relating to one another?
   - Who is important in the image? How do you know?

3. Look at the image as a whole. Make connections to any text that appears with the image.
   - Are there any other important details?
   - What can you figure out about why the image was created?
   - How does the image help you interpret any text?

Europeans treated trade simply as a business activity. The goal of trading was to make money for themselves and their country.

This painting is called *In the Trading Room* and is by Charles William Jefferys. Created in the 1900s, it shows a Mi'kmaq bringing beaver furs to trade for European goods at the French settlement of Port Royal.

Explore and Apply

1. Reread the quotation from the Innu chief on page 162. What do you think it means? What questions do you have about the quotation?

2. Follow the steps in this Toolbox to interpret and analyze one section from this chapter, including its images. What new understanding do you have?

Chapter 8 Fur Trade in Eastern Canada

How Did the Fur Trade Develop?

In the early 1600s, the French began to build trading posts along the St. Lawrence River. King Louis XIII of France decided that a colony should be built to control trade. French people were only allowed to trade for furs if they had a licence from the king. Licences were given to fur traders who promised to build settlements.

This map shows some of the French fur-trading posts in the 1600s. Why do you think the French located the posts where they did?

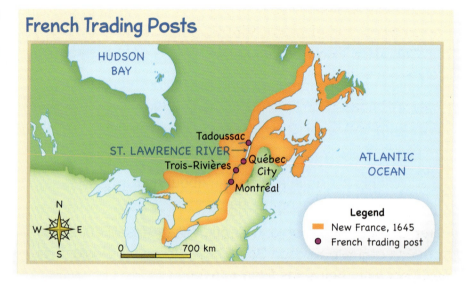

Coureurs de Bois

To get furs, some young French men began to travel deep into unmapped parts of early Canada. These men did not have licences from the king. They were not interested in building settlements. These men were called *coureurs de bois*. **Coureurs de bois** means "runners of the woods." Coureurs de bois did not wait for First Nations trappers to come to them with furs.

These French men met and became friends with First Nations peoples. Coureurs de bois often wintered with First Nations in their camps. They learned their customs and how to survive on the land.

This artwork by Charles William Jeffreys shows a coureur de bois at a First Nations camp in 1660. How does Jefferys view the relationship between the coureurs de bois and First Nations peoples? Support your answer.

Pierre-Esprit Radisson and Médard Chouart des Groseilliers

In 1659, two French coureurs de bois, Pierre-Esprit Radisson and Médard Chouart des Groseilliers, explored the area north of Lake Superior. They had learned from First Nations peoples that there were large populations of beavers to the north. They explored all the way north to what would become Hudson Bay and saw that the area was rich in beavers. They returned to the French fort at Trois-Rivières with 60 canoes loaded with furs. However, they were fined for obtaining furs without a trading licence. Their furs were taken away.

Angry at the French, Radisson and Chouart des Groseilliers sailed to England. They convinced a group of English merchants to support them on a return voyage to Hudson Bay. They explained that their ships could sail directly into Hudson Bay. By sailing into Hudson Bay, the English merchants could avoid conflict with the French who had settled along the St. Lawrence River. In 1668, Radisson and Chouart des Groseilliers sailed from England into Hudson Bay. They returned to England the next year with their ships filled with furs.

This painting shows First Nations guides helping Radisson and Chouart des Groseilliers. It was created by Frederic Remington in 1905.

The Hudson's Bay Company

Radisson and Chouart des Groseilliers' success convinced King Charles II that great wealth could be made from the fur trade. English fur traders began heading to the Hudson Bay area.

In 1670, King Charles II created the Hudson's Bay Company and claimed all the land around Hudson Bay and the rivers that flowed into the bay. He named the land Rupert's Land. The English began setting up trading posts. They were now able to compete with the French for furs.

First Nations peoples had no say in the creation of Rupert's Land. As well, the French did not believe that the English had the right to Rupert's Land. This led to many years of fierce battles between these nations.

Here and Now
The Hudson's Bay Company was in the fur trade for more than 300 years. It stopped trading for furs in 1991. The company exists today as a chain of department stores.

Rupert's Land, Late 1600s

Thinking about Patterns and Trends
Use the map on this page to compare the locations of the French and English trading posts. What patterns do you notice connected to where trading posts were located?

Voyageurs

Because the English created the Hudson's Bay Company, the French faced more competition. They needed to find a way to continue obtaining furs from First Nations farther inland as well as a way to control the fur trade. In 1681, the French passed a law that allowed fur traders to travel directly to meet First Nations peoples. However, traders still needed a licence to do this.

Those who had a licence were called **voyageurs**.
The voyageurs took French goods to First Nations trappers.
They then brought the furs back to the French trading posts.

This painting is called *Canadian Voyageurs Walking a Canoe Up a Rapid*. The painting was created by William Henry Bartlett around 1840. How do you think Bartlett viewed voyageur life? Support your answer.

Did You Know?
In Mattice, Ontario, there is a large statue called the *Missinaibi Traveller*. Mattice is on the Missinaibi River, a fur-trading route. The statue was made to honour the thousands of men who travelled the Missinaibi River carrying trade goods and furs. Many lost their lives on the journey.

Continued Competition

The competition for fur and land in Canada was part of a much larger conflict between France and England. For centuries, the two countries had been in conflict with one another. In Canada, battles raged for many years between the English and French. They often raided each other's trading posts and settlements. Finally, in 1713, the two countries signed a peace agreement called the Treaty of Utrecht. As part of the Treaty of Utrecht, Rupert's Land and some areas of North America claimed by the French went to the English.

Canadians still celebrate and honour our fur-trading past. In this photo, an artist in Winnipeg, Manitoba, creates a snow sculpture of the voyageurs.

Explore and Apply

1. Why do you think the king of France wanted traders to have licences?
2. Create a map of Canada. On your map, show where you would put a trading post. Explain your choice.

Toolbox: Analyze Historical Maps

Historical Maps

A historical map

- is an artifact that shows a particular area at a specific time
- helps us to understand how the world was viewed at that time by the cartographer
- was created using the tools and knowledge available at that time

1 Examine the historical map and read any information that appears with it. Ask yourself: What places do I recognize?

2 Identify who created the map and why. Ask yourself: When was it created? How can I tell what was important to the cartographer? This information will help you understand the perspective of the cartographer.

3 Compare the historical map to modern maps or to satellite images of the same area.

This is a historical map drawn by Samuel de Champlain in 1632. Usually, a cartographer would draw a map from a ship's deck or a canoe. For this map, Champlain did not visit all the places shown, but used the knowledge of First Nations peoples and fur traders. How can you tell from the map what places Champlain actually visited?

Inquiry
Interpret and Analyze

Satellite Images

Today, we have satellites and computers to help us construct maps and more accurate images of Earth's surface.

Compare the historical map and the satellite image.

- How does the size of James Bay on the satellite image differ from the historical map?
- Why are the Great Lakes shaped differently on Champlain's map?

This is a satellite image of the eastern part of Canada.

Explore and Apply

1. How does this historical map help us to understand how Champlain saw this land? How might a satellite image have changed his view?

2. From memory, construct a map of your school's neighbourhood. Check the Internet for a satellite image of the area. Edit and correct your map. How does this exercise compare to the experience of the early mapmakers?

Chapter 8 Fur Trade in Eastern Canada

What Were Some Consequences of the Fur Trade?

Dependence on European Goods

At first, trade benefited both First Nations and Europeans. First Nations peoples valued European metal goods because they were stronger and more durable than those tools that they made from wood, stone, and bone. Fur traders and merchants made a great deal of money selling the furs.

First Nations peoples began to depend on European products. To continue getting these goods, they spent most of their time trapping beaver and transporting furs over long distances. As a result, their traditional way of life began to change. Many First Nations peoples did not have time to hunt and fish in their own communities. As well, some European goods, such as guns and alcohol, proved destructive over time.

This artwork of a Mi'kmaq camp was created around 1850 by an unknown artist. Even though this artwork is from the later years of the fur trade, it shows the types of changes that First Nations in the early years of the trade would also have experienced. Identify the European items that you see. How do you think these items affected the Mi'kmaq?

Thinking about Cause and Consequence

Before reading this section, predict some of the consequences of the fur trade. Preview the headings on pages 170 to 173. What do the headings suggest to you? Begin a cause-and-effect graphic organizer to show your ideas. Add notes to your graphic organizer as you read.

Catholic Connection

Goods are not the only valuable trade items; ideas and knowledge are just as important. In 1610, Jesuit priests came to what is now Port Royal, Nova Scotia. They learned the language of the Mi'kmaq and taught the Mi'kmaq the Catholic faith.

Increased Competition among First Nations Peoples

Traditionally, First Nations peoples did not share the European concept of land ownership. As the fur trade developed, First Nations began to compete with each other for territory and trade. The competition for furs led to many disputes between nations. For example, the Cree and the Dene in the Hudson Bay area competed with each other to trade with the English.

In the early 1700s, a Dene woman, Thanadelthur, helped bring peace between her people and the Cree. She also helped to create a trade alliance between the Dene and the English. This painting of Thanadelthur is called *Ambassadress of Peace*. It was created by Franklin Arbuckle in 1952. Thanadelthur died at the age of 20 from fever.

Land Gain and Land Loss

France and England claimed lands without recognizing that First Nations peoples already lived there. For example, when the English claimed Rupert's Land in 1670, they did not make any treaties with First Nations peoples who lived there.

As the fur trade grew, more and more Europeans arrived. Settlements grew around these posts. First Nations peoples began to lose their traditional hunting grounds.

Alliances and Conflict

The French and the English formed alliances with different First Nations peoples. However, these alliances often led to conflict. For example, Champlain formed trading alliances with the Wendat, Algonkin, and Innu. Champlain agreed to support the Wendat in their ongoing battles and raids against the Haudenosaunee. In 1609, Champlain and the French joined in battle against the Haudenosaunee, killing three chiefs. This caused the Haudenosaunee and the French to become bitter enemies.

Meanwhile, the Haudenosaunee had trading alliances first with the Dutch and later with the English. By the 1640s, they had obtained guns from the Dutch and used them to invade the territory of the Wendat and French fur-trading posts.

Raids and warfare went on for years. By 1700, thousands of people were dead. First Nations peoples and the French began to seek peace. In 1701, a peace treaty was signed among 40 different First Nations and the French. It is called The Great Peace of Montréal.

Champlain sketched this 1609 battle scene between the Wendat and the Haudenosaunee. He sketched himself in the middle of the image. Do you think this is a reliable account of what happened? Why, or why not? Support your answer.

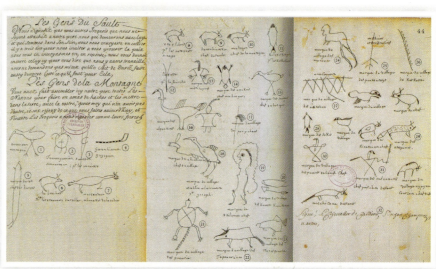

This document shows the signed peace treaty between First Nations and the French. First Nations leaders used the symbols of their clans.

Some First Nations women and European fur traders had children together. Many of these women raised the children on their own when the European fur traders abandoned them and went back to Europe or to their settlements.

During the early 1700s, many of their descendants took part in the fur trade and lived near trading posts. Their knowledge of different cultures made them valuable as guides, interpreters, and clerks.

Diseases

Europeans brought new diseases to Canada. First Nations peoples had never been exposed to these diseases. Their bodies were unable to fight them. Smallpox and measles spread quickly through First Nations populations and killed thousands. Some communities were almost destroyed. This caused many First Nations peoples to distrust Europeans.

Here and Now

In the 1800s, as the fur trade moved farther west, the descendants of First Nations women and French voyageurs came to be known as Métis. Métis helped shape the history of Canada. Today, Métis are recognized as a distinct Aboriginal group.

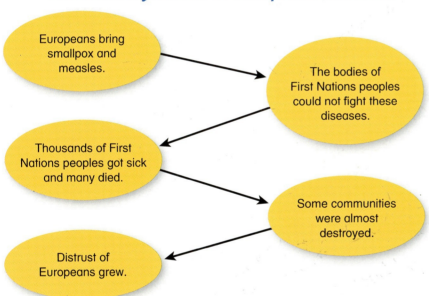

The Consequences of European Diseases

- Europeans bring smallpox and measles.
- The bodies of First Nations peoples could not fight these diseases.
- Thousands of First Nations peoples got sick and many died.
- Some communities were almost destroyed.
- Distrust of Europeans grew.

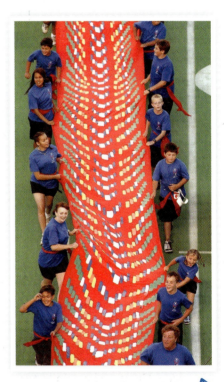

This modern photo shows Métis children carrying a giant sash. During the fur trade, Métis voyageurs wore a sash around their waist. They used the sash for many purposes, including as a rope, towel, and bandage. Today, the sash is an important Métis symbol.

Explore and Apply

1. Which consequence of the fur trade do you think had the greatest significance for First Nations? for Europeans?

2. Create a final draft of the graphic organizer you started on page 170 for Thinking about Cause and Consequence. Use it to help you write a paragraph that answers the following question: Who benefited more from the fur trade, First Nations peoples or Europeans?

Chapter 8 Fur Trade in Eastern Canada

Spotlight on the Beaver

Before the 1500s, more than 60 million beavers lived in the ponds and rivers of Canada. First Nations peoples trapped beavers for food and furs. They only hunted for animals that they needed for survival.

This is a storage room for fur at the reconstructed settlement of Port Royal in Nova Scotia. At Port Royal, the Mi'kmaq not only traded beaver furs but also the furs of other animals, such as fox, bear, otter, raccoon, and lynx.

Declining Beaver Populations

Trapping practices changed during the fur trade. Trappers caught as many beavers as possible. In some years, as many as 100 000 beaver furs were shipped to Europe. Eventually, beaver populations in certain areas disappeared.

The decline in beaver populations had three important consequences:

1. **Exploration:** Fur traders began to search for beavers deeper into the interior of Canada. Following the river routes shown to them by First Nations peoples, fur traders moved from eastern Canada to the north and west. As they travelled, they charted the lands and waterways. Gradually, a map of Canada developed.

2. **Competition:** With fewer beavers left, there was even more competition among fur trappers and traders. This often led to conflict.

3. **Environment:** Beavers live in lodges. To protect their lodges, beavers surround them with dams made from branches, stones, and mud. These dams slow the flow of water and create ponds for plants, fish, birds, muskrats, and other wildlife.

Beaver dams help control flooding downstream. The dams absorb extra water from rain and snowmelt and slowly release it.

Thinking about Continuity and Change

The fur trade continues. However, there are rules to make sure that animals are not over-trapped or over-hunted. What does this change tell you about our society today?

Protecting the Beaver

Over the years, animal protection groups and governments in Canada looked for ways to protect beaver populations. In the 1930s, the federal and provincial governments created strict laws. They limited trapping and required people to get a licence to trap. Beaver populations increased.

Today, Canadian law recognizes the special relationship that First Nations have always had with the land. It honours their right to fish, hunt, and trap year-round. First Nations peoples generally do not require licences to take part in these activities.

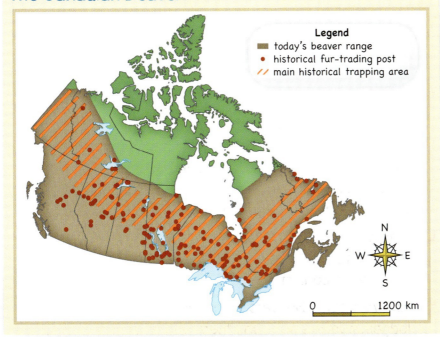

The Canadian Beaver

Faith in Action

Sean Hutton is a student at Holy Trinity Catholic School in Guelph, Ontario. Hutton was worried that warming temperatures are melting the Arctic ice where polar bears live and hunt. This threat to the polar bear threatens the entire Arctic ecosystem. He learned that burning gasoline to run cars is a cause of climate change. So, Hutton organized a walk-to-school day at his school.

Beaver hats fell out of fashion in the 1860s and people no longer wanted to wear them. The fur trade declined. What do you think happened as a result?

Explore and Apply

1. In your own words, explain why the beaver was important to Europeans and First Nations peoples. Next, explain why protecting the beaver is important.

2. Research a Canadian animal that is threatened or endangered. What are the causes? What, if anything, is being done to protect the animal?

Pulling It Together

Father Mike Explains...

The goods of this Earth are God's gift to humanity. Trade serves the common good when it makes it possible for all those involved to get what they need. Trade is unfair when it works against all people getting what they need.

See

Trade is not always fair, especially when the parties involved are unequal in bargaining power. What examples can you give to show this?

Reflect

Catholic social teaching sees greed as a major cause of unfair trade. What do you think this means?

Act

Research the business practice of fair trade. What single action can you take to promote fair trade?

How Can Trade Help the Common Good?

I didn't know how important the fur trade was to Canada's history. First Nations peoples and Europeans worked together to make the fur trade successful. Through trade, they each received important ideas and goods.

I wonder if the trade became less fair to First Nations peoples as time went by.

Our teacher says that trade can have many benefits. It provides jobs. It can help improve people's lives. It can help countries prosper. I believe trade should be fair and everyone should benefit equally.

Aran

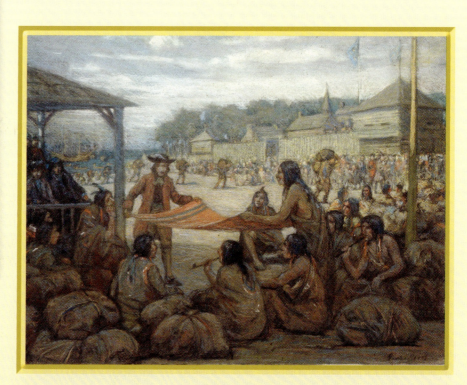

This painting, created by George Agnew Reid in 1916, shows First Nations peoples and the French trading in Montréal.

Summarizing

Create a shape poem to summarize a few important consequences of the fur trade in early Canada. The shape that you choose should represent something from the fur trade.

Making Connections

The fur trade was a competitive business for France and England. What examples of competition do you see in your own community? How do you think competition between stores affects what you buy and how much you pay for it? Reflect on how your answers to these questions increase your understanding of the fur trade.

Pope Paul VI said ...

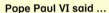 Freedom of trade is fair only if it is subject to the demands of social justice.

On the Development of Peoples (no. 59)

Chapter Inquiry

At the beginning of this chapter, you considered the Big Question: How did the early fur trade affect the relationship between First Nations and Europeans?

Use the information and maps in this chapter to help you interpret and analyze the consequences of the fur trade and the relationships that developed. Remember the steps suggested in the Toolboxes in this chapter. Identify the information that will help you answer the Big Question.

Complete a graphic organizer to help you interpret and analyze information. Share your graphic organizer with a partner. Outline your next steps to continue this inquiry.

Chapter 9

Early Settlements in New France
1604–1713

Big Question

How did early European settlements affect First Nations peoples?

Learning Goals

- identify offices and institutions in New France
- evaluate evidence and draw conclusions
- describe aspects of early contact between First Nations peoples and European settlers in New France

Hi, I'm Geneviève.

I live in Montréal, Québec, near the St. Lawrence River.

Last week in school, we made a family tree. I talked to my parents about my ancestors. I learned that some of my family came to this area in the 1600s. They farmed a plot of land along the St. Lawrence River, near Montréal. It was called Ville-Marie back then.

My ancestors also fished the St. Lawrence River and tapped maple trees for syrup. Every spring, my family still heads out to the sugar camp to help my cousins collect sap.

I wonder what it was like to start a new community. How did my French ancestors get along with First Nations peoples already living in the area?

Francis Back created this painting in 1992. It is his interpretation of what Ville-Marie might have been like in 1685.

Our Faith

The Bible says …

"How very good and pleasant it is when kindred live together in unity!"

Psalm 133 (NRSV)

178 Many Gifts Unit 2

Why Did the French Want to Settle in Canada?

In the 1600s, the French began to build settlements in Canada for the following reasons:

- French rulers wanted to gain power and wealth by claiming lands and resources around the world. To protect and control these claims, they established colonies.

- French rulers and churches wanted to spread Christianity around the world, so the Catholic Church sent missionaries to the colonies to teach Aboriginal peoples about their Catholic faith.

Many of the French people who came to Canada did so because they wanted to make a better life for themselves.

All the lands that the French claimed in North America became known as New France. In claiming these lands, the French did not consider the rights of Aboriginal peoples.

Catholic Connection

Missionaries are people who teach their faith to others. Missionaries today continue the work of Jesus, who said, "I must proclaim the good news of the kingdom of God … for I was sent for this purpose." (Luke 4:43, NRSV)

Settlements in New France

This map shows parts of New France at two different times. Acadia was a territory of New France. Compare this map to the map on page 114. Which First Nations peoples do you think had the most interactions with early settlers? Why do you think so?

Explore and Apply

1. Develop three inquiry questions that you would like to find answers to in this chapter.

2. Predict the challenges that early settlers might have faced in New France. Create a mind map to show your ideas.

Where Were the First Settlements in New France?

Acadia

In 1603, King Henry IV of France granted Pierre Du Gua de Monts full control of the fur trade. In return, de Monts was to establish a colony. Samuel de Champlain sailed to North America with him. They formed their first settlements in an area they named Acadie (Acadia, in English). The settlers who came to live there were eventually called Acadians.

Île Sainte-Croix

Champlain and de Monts first landed on an island they called Île Sainte-Croix. They tried to build a settlement there, but it proved to be a poor location. The island was not sheltered from high coastal winds. The land was not good for farming, and there was little fresh water available. Many people died from scurvy during the first winter.

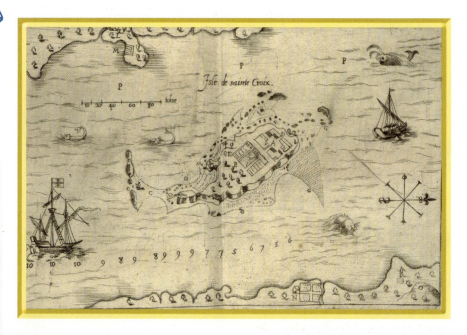

Champlain created this map of Île Sainte-Croix in 1613. Based on this map, why do you think Pierre Du Gua de Monts and Champlain thought that this would be a good location for a settlement?

Here and Now

Some of the French settlers in Port Royal married Mi'kmaq women. The settlers liked how the Mi'kmaq made decisions. The Mi'kmaq made sure everyone agreed with decisions. Their descendants still live in the area. The language of the Acadians is French combined with Mi'kmaq words.

Port Royal

In the spring of 1605, de Monts moved the settlement to a more sheltered area. He called it Port Royal. The settlers cleared the land and planted wheat, barley, and vegetables. The forests provided them with firewood, logs to build houses, and animals to hunt.

The French settlers developed good relations with the Mi'kmaq. The Mi'kmaq traded furs with the settlers and helped them survive the cold winters. The two groups developed a friendship that grew into an alliance against the English. The English had their own colonies to the south, in what is now the United States.

For a few years, Port Royal seemed to be successful. However, the fur trade was not making money for France. In 1607, King Henry IV took away the full control that he had granted de Monts to trade for furs. This allowed others to start trading furs in Acadia. De Monts believed that Port Royal would not survive with the added competition. He returned to France with some of the settlers. In 1613, the English burned Port Royal to the ground in a battle for the area.

Battling for Acadia

For the next 150 years, France and England battled for control of lands in North America, including Acadia. Acadia was located in a strategic position. It was close to valuable fishing waters, and its territory included the Gulf of St. Lawrence. All ships sailing into the St. Lawrence River had to pass through the gulf. This meant that whoever controlled the gulf had control over shipping traffic.

In 1713, after France and England signed the Treaty of Utrecht, much of Acadia and other North American lands came under England's rule.

Throughout the conflict, the Acadians wanted to live in peace. In 1755, the English tried to force them to be loyal to England. When the Acadians refused, the English forced them out of Acadia. Many Acadians went to different parts of the world. In 1764, some returned to Acadia.

Mi'kmaq Chief Membertou welcomed the French settlers. In 1610, he was believed to be the first person among First Nations peoples to be baptized. At his baptism, he took the name Henri, in honour of the French king. For three years after de Monts left Port Royal, the chief looked after the settlement. He was honoured with a postage stamp in 2007.

The modern Mi'kmaq artist Alan Syliboy created this painting, called *Membertou*, to honour Chief Membertou. Syliboy says that the chief was baptized to help build good relations with the French. Having good relations benefited both the Mi'kmaq and the French.

Québec

In 1607, Champlain left Port Royal and sailed back to France. He was certain that a French colony could develop in North America, so he returned to Canada the following year. He arrived with two ships of settlers to carry out his plan.

Champlain decided to build a settlement along the shores of the St. Lawrence River. He chose a location where the First Nations village of Stadacona once stood. By settling there, Champlain could continue to be involved in the fur trade, as well as explore farther west. He called the settlement Québec. The name came from the Algonkian word *Kebec*, meaning "where the river narrows." Today, this city is known as Québec City.

Champlain had the settlers build a large wooden fort on the site. It was located near water and sat high on a cliff. This location provided protection from enemy attacks. The land around the fort was suitable for growing crops. Despite this, the first winter was very hard for the settlers. They suffered from scurvy and hunger. Many settlers died.

The fort became a fur-trading post. Champlain understood that the success of the fur trade depended on having good relations with First Nations peoples. He developed trading alliances with the Innu, Algonkin, and Wendat in the area. They shared their trading routes with the French fur traders and provided them with food, furs, and canoes.

Did You Know?

In the 1600s, it took about six to eight weeks to sail from Europe to Canada. Life on ships was difficult. Rough seas and dirty conditions often made passengers sick. People shared crowded, dark, and damp spaces with animals such as pigs, chickens, and sheep. They ate mainly dried biscuits, with some salted meat and a few vegetables.

Champlain created this drawing of the fort at Québec in 1613.

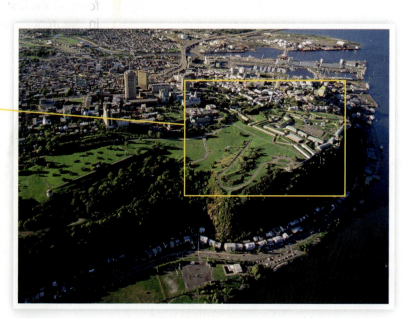

This is a modern-day aerial photo of Québec City. What do you notice? Why do you think both the people of Stadacona and Champlain chose this location for a community?

Champlain tried to persuade the king of France to send more settlers to help the colony to grow. Over the years, the king gave various fur-trading companies control of the fur trade in New France. They were supposed to develop the trade and the colony. However, the companies were more interested in making money than in developing settlements. Therefore, the population of Québec grew very slowly. In 1620, there were only about 60 people living in the settlement.

Ville-Marie

In May 1641, Paul de Chomedy de Maisonneuve sailed from France with the goal of developing settlements along the St. Lawrence River. Jeanne Mance, a French nurse, took part in this effort. Along with about 40 others, they travelled from Québec to the site where the First Nations village of Hochelaga was once located. They built a fort there that they called Ville-Marie.

Early life in Ville-Marie was difficult. The population grew slowly. By 1651, only 50 people lived there.

Catholic Connection

Marguerite Bourgeoys arrived in Ville-Marie in 1653. She opened schools for First Nations children, as well as for children of settlers. She founded the Congregation de Notre-Dame. It was made up of nuns who taught religion, reading, writing, and practical skills. Bourgeoys was made a saint in 1982. She was Canada's first female saint.

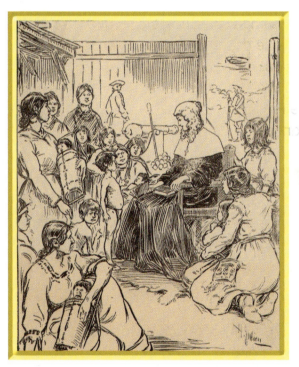

Henri Julien created this artwork sometime between 1880 and 1908. Jeanne Mance is shown with First Nations women and children. In 1645, Mance founded the first hospital in Montréal, called the Hôtel-Dieu.

Here and Now

The Hôtel-Dieu is still operating today. Canada's highest award in nursing is called the Jeanne Mance Award.

Explore and Apply

1. Would you want to live in one of these early settlements? Why, or why not?
2. Create a timeline for settlements in New France.

How Was the Land Divided and Developed in New France?

The Seigneurial System

As New France expanded, the settlers developed their communities in the same way that they did in France. The way they divided land was called the **seigneurial system**.

In this aerial photo from 2007, you can still see how the land was originally developed as narrow strips along the St. Lawrence River.

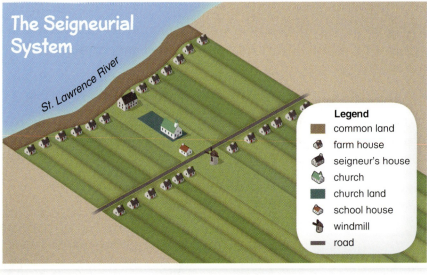

What do you think were the benefits of dividing land in this way?

The Seigneurs

In 1627, the king of France, Louis XIII, granted land along the St. Lawrence River mainly to French nobles. These nobles were called **seigneurs**. In return, the seigneurs vowed to be loyal to the king and promised to bring settlers from France to farm the land. The seigneurs were responsible for dividing the land into lots. They also had to build roads, a church, and a mill in which to grind grain.

The Seigneury

The land that was granted to each seigneur was called a *seigneury*. The earliest seigneuries bordered the St. Lawrence River. Having access to a water source was important for crop irrigation, travel, and food. There was a small strip of land along the shoreline that everyone in the seigneuries could use. From this common area, narrow strips of land ran back from the river. Each piece of land was rented to a settler to farm.

> **Did You Know?**
> Madeleine d'Allonne (1646–1718) was among the first women to hold a seigneury in New France. She also worked for the rights of settlers.

The Habitants

The people who farmed the land called themselves **habitants**. They were usually farmers and labourers from France. The seigneurs required habitants to build homes, clear their land for planting crops, and then farm it.

The habitants also had other important duties. They had to pay taxes in the form of grain and fish to their seigneur. For example, one out of every 14 sacks of wheat ground at the local mill had to be given to the seigneur. Habitants had to work for free on the seigneur's land for three days a year. If they did not fulfill their responsibilities, the seigneur could take back the land.

Life in New France offered the habitants greater opportunities and benefits than their lives in France did. They were able to rent large pieces of land and they paid fewer taxes than they did in their homeland.

Thinking about Perspective

In 1641, about 240 French people lived in New France. About 15 000 Wendat and Haudenosaunee also lived in the area. How might these First Nations peoples have viewed the small French population and their use of the land?

In 1787, Thomas Davies created this painting of a typical seigneury. What connections can you make between the text and this painting?

Explore and Apply

1. In what ways might the relationship between First Nations peoples and fur traders be different from the relationship between First Nations peoples and settlers? Explain your reasoning.

2. Use a graphic organizer to compare how the Wendat and French settlers used the land. Draw conclusions about the differences and similarities.

Chapter 9 Early Settlements in New France

What Was Daily Life Like in New France?

New France was a rural society and the settlers were mostly farmers. Daily life was not easy. First Nations peoples in the area taught settlers many survival skills. Settlers developed a lifestyle that included aspects of First Nations ways.

Families were generally large, often with 10 or more children. Everyone contributed to life on the farm.

The Catholic Church was an important part of daily life for early settlers. They attended Mass weekly. Gathering with neighbours allowed them time to socialize.

> " You note, in the first place, a great love and union [among the Wendat].... Their hospitality towards all sorts of strangers is remarkable.... They never close the door upon a stranger, and, once having received him into their homes, they share with him the best they have.... "

Father Jean de Brébeuf wrote this passage in the 1630s.

This photo from the 1950s shows Sainte-Anne-de-Beaupré cathedral. It was built in the 1600s near Québec City. This cathedral is still important today. Many people with disabilities or illnesses visit this cathedral to pray to be healed.

Faith in Action

In 2013, students at Pope John Paul II Catholic Elementary School in Oakville, Ontario, held a Meet, Greet, and Eat gathering for new immigrant families. It was an opportunity for families new to the community to meet one another.

Men's Roles

For the most part, men cleared the land of trees and rocks, and prepared the soil for planting. Wheat, corn, barley, peas, and oats were some of the crops that were planted in spring and harvested in fall. Crops included those that the settlers learned about from First Nations peoples, such as corn, beans, and squash. In early spring, men tapped maple trees for syrup, a skill they learned from First Nations peoples. Men also cared for and fed the pigs, cows, sheep, and other farm animals. As well, they repaired the home, barns, and farming tools.

Women's Roles

Women generally cared for the home and children. They spun wool and wove it into fabric to make clothing. Women learned to line clothing and boots with fur for extra warmth during winter. They made blankets, rugs, and candles for their homes. Women also looked after the vegetable and herb gardens. They cooked food using the crops that they grew.

First Nations women shared their knowledge with French women. They showed the settlers new ways to preserve food for winter and what plants could be used for medicines.

Children's Roles

Young children also worked hard. They collected firewood, pulled weeds from the garden, and gathered berries from the forest. As they grew up, boys worked alongside their fathers in the fields, and girls learned to cook and look after the home from their mothers.

Lawrence Batchelor created this painting around 1931. It shows a government official visiting a habitant family in the 1660s. What do you learn about a habitant's family life from this painting?

Thinking about Continuity and Change

In some ways, the lives of children in Canada today are similar to those of children in New France. In other ways, they are different. What are the main similarities and differences between your day-to-day life and the life of a child in New France?

Explore and Apply

1. Compare the roles of adults in New France to the roles of adults in Wendat communities before the French came.
2. In role as a habitant (man, woman, or child), write a diary entry or letter describing a typical day in New France.

How Was New France Governed?

In 1663, King Louis XIV of France wanted to secure his claim to New France and see it grow. He realized that the future of the colony depended on increasing its population. He took control of the colony from the fur-trading company, which was interested only in the fur trade. The king created the Sovereign Council, which included three positions: governor, intendant, and bishop.

Expanding the Colony

The first intendant in New France was Jean Talon. To help the population grow, he brought single, young women to marry fur traders and farmers. Many of these women were orphans. The French king paid for their journey to New France. For this reason, these women were called *filles du roi*, or the "king's daughters."

Government Positions and Responsibilities

Position	Responsibilities
Governor	• govern in the name of the king • provide defence
Intendant	• run day-to-day business of colony • manage wealth and resources, including fur trade • settle disputes
Bishop	• lead the Church • build hospitals and schools

Did You Know?

Jean Talon encouraged people to marry young and have large families. The government even gave money to encourage this. In 1663, the population of New France was about 2500. By 1673, it was more than 6700.

Between 1663 and 1673, around 800 filles du roi arrived in New France. In 1927, Eleanor Fortescue Brickdale created this painting of the arrival of the filles du roi.

Explore and Apply

1. Why do you think it was difficult to get the French to come to New France?

2. Create a graphic organizer to show the causes that led to the coming of the filles du roi, as well as the consequences. Include both a cause and a consequence that go beyond what you are told in the text.

Why Did Missionaries Come to New France?

Missionaries began to arrive in 1611. They provided for the spiritual welfare of settlers and helped establish hospitals and schools. They also taught First Nations peoples about the Catholic faith and French culture. The French government believed that having First Nations peoples adopt Catholicism and French culture would make them loyal to France. Building this loyalty would help France compete against England for land and furs.

In 1625, Jesuit priests, including Father Jean de Brébeuf, arrived in Québec. Father Brébeuf began his missionary work with the Innu who lived in the area. Soon, he was assigned to work with the Wendat in the area of present-day Georgian Bay.

In 1639, the Ursuline nuns arrived in New France. Their calling was to educate girls, including First Nations girls. The nuns established convents and schools, and taught reading, writing, religion, and homemaking skills. Their religious order still exists today.

> I am greatly astonished that the French have so little cleverness ... in the effort to persuade us to convert our poles, our barks, and our wigwams into those houses of stone and of wood.... Do we not find in our own [shelters] all the conveniences and the advantages that you have with yours ... ?

This quotation was part of a speech by a Mi'kmaq Elder to a group of French settlers in 1677. The speech was recorded in a book by Father Chrestien Le Clercq. What do you learn about how some of the Mi'kmaq might have viewed the French?

Missionaries thought they were helping First Nations peoples by teaching them their faith and European ways. Over time, some First Nations peoples lost their own spiritual beliefs, languages, and cultures partly because of the work of missionaries.

Lawrence Batchelor created this painting in 1931. It shows Ursuline nuns with First Nations girls. Whose perspective does this painting show? Use evidence to support your answer.

Explore and Apply

1. Explain how a First Nations shaman would view the missionaries. Support your ideas.
2. Do you think the coureurs de bois, the settlers, and the missionaries viewed First Nations peoples in the same way? Create a chart to show your ideas.

Spotlight on Sainte-Marie among the Hurons

The Mission Is Built

In 1639, Jesuit missionaries built a mission near what is now Midland, Ontario. The mission was called Sainte-Marie among the Hurons. *Huron* is the French word for Wendat. The mission was built in the heart of Wendat fur-trading territory.

Father Jérome Lalemant and Father Brébeuf led the missionaries. Their goal was to use the mission as a central base. From there, they would travel to Wendat villages and spread the Catholic faith. Sainte-Marie among the Hurons was the first European settlement in what is now Ontario.

In the 1960s, archaeologists working for the Ontario government helped to reconstruct the mission at its original site. They did not rebuild everything that was on the original site. They made choices that reflect what they believed was most important or interesting.

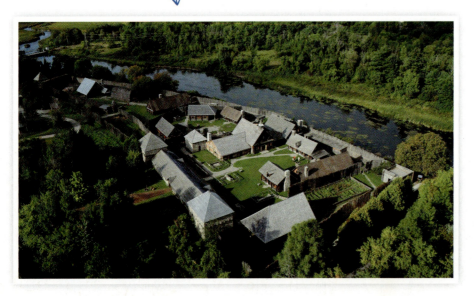

Over the years, a number of Jesuit priests and other men arrived at the mission. No women were at the mission. The men who came included carpenters, blacksmiths, and soldiers. They helped to build, run, and protect the mission as it grew. By 1648, 66 French people lived in the mission—one-fifth of the European population of New France.

Sainte-Marie among the Hurons

The Mission Site

The Jesuits wanted to make Sainte-Marie among the Hurons a permanent and safe mission. They located the mission on the Wye River because the river provided a water route for them to visit the smaller missions in the area. The river also supplied fresh water. For food, the people at the mission planted vegetable and herb gardens. Livestock was brought from Québec by canoe. To protect the mission from harsh weather and Haudenosaunee attacks, the settlers constructed a wooden fence around the buildings.

The Jesuits divided the mission into two sections. In one area were their residences, their chapel, a cookhouse, and a carpenter's shop. The other area of the mission had a chapel, a hospital, and two longhouses for those Wendat who were learning about the Catholic faith.

This photo shows a part of the reconstructed mission. How did the natural environment and the structures missionaries built help them meet their needs?

Tension between Societies

The Wendat and missionaries were generally friendly with each other. However, there was sometimes tension and even conflict between the two groups of people.

Many Wendat were suspicious of the missionaries. They did not understand why the Jesuits did not recognize the Wendat's spiritual beliefs. Sometimes, this led to misunderstandings.

The Wendat were also fearful of contact because Europeans brought infectious diseases, such as smallpox and measles. These diseases swept through Wendat villages, killing thousands. Approximately two-thirds of the Wendat population died in just a few years. Many Wendat blamed the Jesuits for their illnesses.

Even though they were suspicious and fearful, many Wendat converted to Catholicism. Some converted to get goods from the French. Others converted because they thought it would help trading relations with the French. Many of these Wendat went back to their own beliefs and practices when they left the mission. This often frustrated the Jesuits. Other Wendat did not convert at all. This led to tensions within Wendat communities.

Catholic Connection

Saint Kateri Tekakwitha was a Mohawk woman who died in 1680, when she was 24 years old. For her devotion to the sick, she was made a saint in 2012. She is the patron saint of the environment and ecology.

Her father was a chief who converted to Catholicism. Her mother was also Catholic and educated by French missionaries. Her parents died from smallpox when she was 4 years old.

This is a reconstruction of the chapel at Sainte-Marie among the Hurons. Compare the interior of this chapel to churches you know.

As well, the presence of the French in the area increased the conflict between the Wendat and Haudenosaunee. The two First Nations had been in conflict for a long time. Rivalry between them grew during the fur trade as they formed different alliances with the French and the English. The Wendat were allied with the French and the Haudenosaunee were allied with the English.

The Mission Is Burned

In 1648, the Haudenosaunee launched attacks on Wendat villages. Weakened by disease, the Wendat could not defend themselves, and many were killed. Several Jesuit priests, including Father Brébeuf, were killed during these attacks.

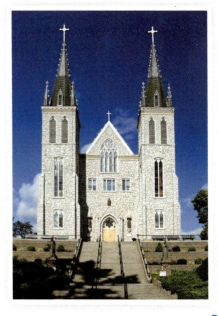

In June 1649, fearing further raids, the remaining Jesuits burned the mission to the ground. They and many of the Wendat travelled to nearby St. Joseph Island (now Christian Island) in Georgian Bay to start a new mission. They spent a difficult winter there. Many died of starvation or from attacks by the Haudenosaunee. The next summer, the remaining Jesuits and a few hundred Wendat returned to Québec.

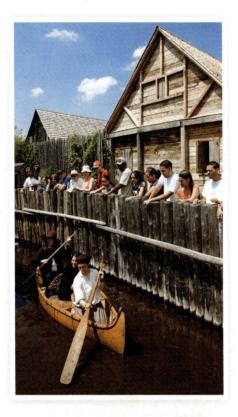

Across the road from Sainte-Marie among the Hurons is a site called the Martyrs' Shrine. It is a national shrine to eight Jesuit missionaries who died for their faith. These men were recognized as saints in 1930. Today, thousands of pilgrims visit the shrine each year.

Today, visitors go to Sainte-Marie among the Hurons to learn about life at the mission.

Explore and Apply

1. Was Sainte-Marie among the Hurons a successful mission? Explain why you think so.
2. Create an information card or pamphlet for tourists visiting Sainte-Marie among the Hurons. What historical information and images will you include on your card? How will you convey the significance of this historical site?

Toolbox: Evaluate Evidence and Draw Conclusions

Evaluating and Drawing Conclusions

Evaluating means making reasoned judgments about what is most important. As you evaluate, it is important to consider the perspectives of the various groups involved. A sound conclusion is a statement that can be proved. Facts are used to build proof. Our values also play a big part in evaluating and drawing conclusions.

1. Decide what information will be most useful to help you answer your question.
2. Consider whether you can trust the source.
3. Look for patterns and relationships to connect the information in a meaningful way.
4. Develop summary statements to show your understanding.
5. Use these statements to help you draw conclusions supported by facts that answer your inquiry question.

Geneviève read the question on page 193: "Was Sainte-Marie among the Hurons a successful mission? Explain why you think so." She wanted to answer that question. Geneviève gathered information from the Spotlight on pages 190 to 193. She also found this painting. She followed the above steps to evaluate and draw conclusions.

Vernon Mould created this painting of Sainte-Marie among the Hurons in 1967. Before 1600, about 25 000 Wendat lived in the area. By the time the mission was burned down in 1649, only a few thousand Wendat remained. Most had died from European diseases or battles with the Haudenosaunee.

Inquiry
Evaluate and Draw Conclusions

Geneviève created this chart to help her organize her observations and ideas.

Successful or Unsuccessful?

Findings about the Mission	Positive	Negative
It was built to spread the Catholic faith.	The missionaries were welcomed into First Nations communities.	The missionaries ignored the traditional faith of the Wendat.
It extended French influence westward.	The mission was in the Georgian Bay area, moving westward.	The mission was very far from other French communities.
It included a hospital to nurse the sick.	This could have helped some First Nations peoples.	Diseases destroyed Wendat communities.
It was the first European settlement in Ontario.	The mission could be used as a stepping stone for western travel.	After the mission was attacked in 1649, the remaining priests and Wendat burned the mission to the ground.
The mission ran for 10 years.	The Wendat and the missionaries established friendly relationships.	The mission was under constant threat and attack. Missionaries decided to burn it down and go back to Québec.

Thinking about Significance

Historical sites, such as Sainte-Marie among the Hurons, are sometimes preserved and rebuilt. Why is the mission significant to Canadian history?

Geneviève used her observations and the chart to draw conclusions. To make her conclusions stronger, she considered the perspective of each group involved.

Explore and Apply

1. What conclusions do you think Geneviève drew? What supports her conclusions?
2. What other observations can you make about Sainte-Marie among the Hurons? In your notebook, create a new row for the chart above. Evaluate and draw conclusions to answer the question about the success of the mission.

How Are Relationships of the Past Related to Issues Today?

When Europeans first came to Canada, they claimed the land as their own, despite the presence of First Nations peoples. As the French and English competed to claim and settle land, they made alliances with First Nations. Eventually, they signed treaties with some of them.

Different Views of Treaties

For First Nations peoples, treaties were made for peace, friendship, and trade. They recognized treaties as sacred and lasting forever. For example, the Haudenosaunee Confederacy was formed one thousand years ago. The Confederacy still exists today. Its constitution, the Great Law of Peace, is still respected. In 1701, 40 First Nations signed the Great Peace of Montréal with New France. Those nations continue to celebrate this agreement.

Faith in Action

Harnoor Gill is a student at Christ the King Catholic Secondary School in Georgetown, Ontario. He started the Peace Welcome Club to encourage immigrants, ages 4 to 18, to learn about their communities and contribute to them. Gill believes that everyone "can be peace-community builders."

Tsaminik Rankin, an Algonkin spiritual leader, uses a peace pipe during a 2001 ceremony celebrating the 300th anniversary of the Great Peace of Montréal.

However, the idea of signing a treaty to decide who owned the land was a European idea. Often, treaties took away much of First Nations peoples' traditional lands and many of their rights, such as where they could hunt and fish. First Nations peoples did not understand the European idea of land ownership. They believed that people were part of the land, and that the land was meant to be shared. As well, many later governments ignored or did not respect treaties signed by First Nations groups and governments in the past.

Land Claims

Today, many land disputes still need to be settled. First Nations use a process called a **land claim** to have their rights to certain territories recognized.

Land claims are quite complicated and hard to settle. For example, Mohawks of Kanesatake and the townspeople of Oka, near Montréal, are still working to settle a land dispute from the 1700s. In the early 1700s, the governor of New France granted land in this area to a missionary community. The governor had previously granted the same land to the Mohawks.

For almost 300 years, there were disputes. In 1990, the Mohawks protested plans by the town of Oka to expand a golf course and housing project. These projects would cover their ancestors' burial ground. This protest led to clashes and a tense standoff that lasted for more than two months.

Since then, the Canadian government has tried to deal with land claims peacefully. It is trying to build better relations with First Nations peoples. First Nations leaders believe that much more work needs to be done. About 800 land claims still need to be resolved.

Mohawk supporter Brad Larocque (right) faces soldier Patrick Cloutier during the Oka standoff. Can differing perspectives benefit a country or do they simply cause conflict? Explain.

Explore and Apply

1. How is the history of First Nations and European interactions hundreds of years ago relevant to Canadians today? Explain.

2. Create a slogan and logo to reflect nations working together for peace.

Pulling It Together

Father Mike Explains...

If you look at an image of Earth taken from space, you can see that we are all together on this Earth. Most people who migrate from one country to another do so out of need, for example, to be safe.

See

When people of different cultures come together, it can give rise to conflict or lead to cooperation as they learn from one another. Look for examples of cooperation around you.

Reflect

What does our history teach us about the need for people to live and work together peaceably?

Act

Create a posting for your school website that welcomes newcomers and encourages working together within the school community.

How Does Respecting People's Rights Serve the Common Good?

I learned that many settlers came to Canada to make a better life for themselves. They worked hard to build a new life and new communities. Today, immigrants also come to build a new and better life. My best friend, Mercy, came here after the typhoon in the Philippines in 2013. She and her family lost their home.

I learned that settlers often didn't think about or respect First Nations peoples' rights. My mom says that we all need to work together to respect everyone's rights. When we do this, we help build a stronger and safer country.

Geneviève

This photo was taken in 2013. It shows Attawapiskat Chief Theresa Spence (lower left) with supporters. She is on her way to speak with Governor General David Johnston about the rights of First Nations peoples.

Summarizing

You have been asked to write the back cover copy for a book about settlers in early New France. Use your learning in this chapter to write a short blurb.

Making Connections

List the connections that you can make to the lives of early settlers and your own life. How do the connections help you to understand and appreciate how Canada has changed?

The Bible says …

"How very good and pleasant it is when kindred live together in unity!"
Psalm 133 (NRSV)

Chapter Inquiry

Develop an inquiry question related to this chapter or use the Big Question: How did early European settlements affect First Nations peoples?

Gather information to answer the question. How will you organize the information?

Use your information to evaluate and draw conclusions. Write a conclusion statement and share it with a partner.

Unit Inquiry

Investigating First Nations Peoples and Europeans in Early Canada

At the beginning of Unit 2: First Nations and European Explorers, you were asked to become an archaeologist to dig into Canada's past. You will now complete your inquiry into the interactions between groups of people in early Canada. For example, you might explore the relationship between the Haudenosaunee and the Wendat or the Vikings and the Beothuk.

You will also examine the perspectives of the different groups. How did group members view the relationship? Did the relationship work toward the common good?

Formulate Questions

Select an early interaction that you want to investigate further. Create a graphic organizer, such as a q-chart, to focus your inquiry.

Choose three probing questions to guide your inquiry. To help you, look at the Big Question at the beginning of each chapter. Share your questions with your classmates. Provide each other with feedback. If necessary, revise your questions based on the feedback.

Checklist

I will develop questions to guide my research that help me

- ☑ think about my learning
- ☑ think deeply about the topic
- ☑ combine ideas
- ☑ draw conclusions

Gather and Organize Information

Review the chapter or chapters in *Many Gifts 5* that explore the interaction you have chosen for your inquiry. You will also need to research information from other sources. Gather a variety of primary and secondary sources. These might include artifacts, oral stories, documentaries, interviews, photos, paintings, websites, and history books.

Create a graphic organizer, such as the one below. Organize the information in a meaningful way that will help you go on to interpret and analyze the information.

Title of Source and Format (e.g., book, map, photo)	Type of Source (primary or secondary)	Who Created the Source and When	What I Learned from the Source (main idea)

Checklist
I will
- ☑ identify the sources I can use
- ☑ compare information from different sources
- ☑ identify the perspective of each source
- ☑ check that I have enough information to answer my questions
- ☑ create an organizer to help me with the next step in my inquiry: interpreting and analyzing

Interpret and Analyze Information

Review the information that you have already gathered and organized. Is anything missing? Where else might you look for information to complete your research?

To interpret and analyze the information you have gathered, think deeply about the impact of the interactions between the two groups of people. Do you have a good understanding of what happened when the groups interacted with each other? Have you looked at the interaction from both perspectives? You might create a graphic organizer to help you organize each perspective.

Checklist
I will
- ☑ determine what is important
- ☑ restate my findings in my own words
- ☑ make connections and identify patterns
- ☑ reflect on any new understandings I have gained based on connections I made or patterns I identified

Checklist

I will

- ☑ evaluate my sources of information for accuracy and for reliability
- ☑ draw conclusions based on the information I researched
- ☑ share my conclusions and supporting evidence with a classmate to see if they are convincing
- ☑ revise my conclusions or supporting evidence if needed

Evaluate and Draw Conclusions

Evaluate the information you have gathered. What conclusions can you draw to answer your inquiry questions? What evidence in your research supports your conclusions?

One way to draw conclusions is to ask yourself questions, such as the following:

- Were all interactions of people in early Canada positive?
- Are any of the interactions between First Nations peoples and Europeans connected to issues in present-day Canada?

Another way to draw conclusions is to complete sentence starters, such as the ones below:

- Based on my research, I can conclude that the fur trade ...
- Based on my research, I can conclude that the Wendat and the French missionaries ...

Extend Your Learning

How does the interaction you researched affect Canadians today? Consider the people's lives before, during, and after this interaction. What conclusions can you draw?

Communicate Your Findings

Think about how you can most effectively present the information and your conclusions. For example, you might

- create a video focusing on a situation, a person, an artifact, or another piece of historical evidence
- write a biography
- write and present a speech
- draw three scenes that show the lives of the people before, during, and after interacting with each other
- write a magazine or online article
- create a photo essay

Be creative! You want your audience to be interested and to learn something about how people interacted long ago.

Reflect on Your Learning

Think about all that you have learned in this inquiry project. What questions do you still have? How effectively did you communicate your findings to your audience? What part of the inquiry process did you find the most challenging?

Checklist

I will

- ☑ present the information in an interesting way
- ☑ use words and visuals to present my conclusions

My presentation will include

- ☑ an opening statement to identify the interaction I have chosen, the timeframe, and the people involved
- ☑ an explanation of how the people interacted with each other
- ☑ a conclusion about the effects of the interaction

Glossary

A

Aboriginal peoples: people who have been living in a land from the earliest times; in Canada, Aboriginal peoples are First Nations, Métis, and Inuit

act: a formal decision, such as a law, made by a court or other authority

active citizenship: to be active in one's community, working toward the common good

allegiance: loyalty toward a person or a country

ally: a person or group who works with others

archaeologist: a scientist who studies peoples of the past by examining their artifacts or by digging into the ground to examine the artifacts found there

artifact: an object that was made long ago

B

ballot: a paper or card that voters use to cast their vote during an election

band: a group of First Nations peoples who live in an area and share a common culture and ancestry

band council: the local government that serves communities on First Nations reserves

bartering: trading of goods for goods, without the use of money

board: a small group of people who help municipal governments manage services and make decisions; may be called a commission or committee

boreal forest: a forest made up of mainly coniferous trees, such as white spruce, black spruce, balsam fir, and jack pine

budget: a plan created by provincial or territorial governments to show how they will spend the money they have raised from taxes or received from the federal government

bylaw: a local rule made by local governments

C

cabinet: a group of elected members who have been chosen by the leader of the party to provide advice and share the responsibilities of governing

cabinet minister: a member of the provincial, territorial, or federal cabinet

candidate: a person who runs for election, hoping to be elected to become part of the government

colonize: to create settlements in a new land in order to control the land and trade in the region

colony: an area claimed and controlled by a country in another part of the world

commission: (*see* board)

committee: (*see* board)

confederacy: a union or alliance between groups; an agreement to work together

consensus: agreement

consensus government: government that reaches decisions by considering the opinions of all members of the assembly

constitution: a document that describes how a country will run and be governed

council (band or municipality): a group of people elected to make decisions for the community

councillor: an elected member of a council

coureurs de bois (runners of the woods): French men who traded for furs with First Nations peoples

D

discrimination: unfair treatment of people because of their race, gender, or beliefs

E

ecosystem: all living and non-living things that exist naturally in an area and depend on one another

Elder: a person in Aboriginal communities who is respected for their great wisdom about their beliefs and culture

elect: to choose someone to govern by voting

election: an event where people elect members of the government by voting

engineer: a person trained to help design buildings and structures so that they are sturdy and safe

executive branch: a part of the federal government made up of the governor general, the prime minister, the cabinet, and all the departments, who together deliver federal services

expedition: a journey that is organized for a specific purpose

exported: when a good is sold to and then shipped to another country

F

federation: a group made up of smaller groups that agree to work together

filles du roi (king's daughters): young French women who came to New France to marry and settle, and whose journey was paid for by the French king

funded: paid for

funds: money

G

goods: items that are made to be bought and sold

govern: to watch over and guide the policies and services of a community, province, territory, or country

government: the system of political control or rule of citizens, communities, or areas

governor general: a representative of the monarch or ruler

H

habitant: a person in New France who farmed the land

Hansard: a word-for-word record of every debate held in the legislature

head of council: the person elected by the community to lead the municipal council

House of Commons: one of the two houses of Canada's Parliament, made up of elected representatives from across Canada

I

immigrant: a person who leaves his or her home country to live permanently in other countries

indigenous peoples: the original peoples of a land

interpreter: someone who understands or explains the meaning of messages that are unclear or in a different language

J

judicial branch: the branch of government responsible for applying and interpreting laws

jurisdiction: the power to make decisions and laws for an area

K

kinship: a tie between people who are related through blood or marriage

L

land claim: to declare ownership of an area; a process First Nations can use to have their rights to certain territories recognized

legislation: a law

legislative branch: the branch of government that creates laws

legislature: a provincial or territorial government, also called the legislative assembly; the building in which a provincial or territorial government meets is also called a legislature

Lieutenant Governor: the monarch's representative in the provinces

local government: a group of people who are elected, or chosen, to make decisions for an area such as a town, city, village, or small region

longhouse: a solid, permanent home made of wood and bark

M

mayor: the head of council in a large centre

member of Parliament: an elected member of the federal government

member of the provincial Parliament: an elected member of the provincial government

merchant: a person who buys and sells goods

Métis: a person whose ancestors include both First Nations and Europeans

missionary: a person who teaches their faith to others

monarch: a king, queen, or ruler

municipal council: a group of people who have been elected to make decisions for a municipality

municipal department: a group of people with special knowledge and skills who deliver services in a particular area

municipality: a community or an area within a province or territory that has its own local government

O

Official Opposition: the political party with the second most members elected

opposition party: a party that has fewer members elected than the government

oral tradition: the passing of knowledge, history, and culture from one generation to the next through spoken words

P

Parliament: the legislative branch of the federal government, which proposes and passes bills

party system: a system of government where candidates running for election are part of a political party

permanent residents: people who live permanently in a country

petroglyphs: a rock carving or rock painting that was created long ago

platform: beliefs of a political party

political party: a team of candidates and leaders that share similar ideas about what is important

premier: leader of the province or territory, who is the leader of the party that has the most members elected

property tax: taxes paid by property owners to help pay for services

provincial Parliament: the legislature of a province

public hearing: a meeting open to everyone

public servant: a person who works for government departments

R

reeve: the head of council in a smaller centre

referendum: a process in which community members vote on whether the government should take a certain action

refugees: people who are forced to move from their country of birth because of the danger or extreme hardship they are experiencing

regional chair: the head of council in a regional municipality

regional municipality: a region that includes more than one municipality

representation by population: a system whereby the number of representatives that each province or territory has in the federal government depends on population

representative: a person who is elected to speak for a particular area

reserve: area of land set aside by a government for the use of Aboriginal peoples

riding: area of a province or territory; each area elects one member to the government

right: the authority or freedom to act or behave in a certain way

S

saga: a long story that tells about heroes, especially those of the Norse

sanctuary: an area reserved for wild animals

seigneur: a French noble

seigneurial system: the way settlers divided the land as New France expanded

seigneury: the land that was granted to each seigneur

Senate: one of the two houses of the Canadian Parliament, made up of members appointed by the prime minister

senator: a member of the senate chosen by the prime minister from a region of Canada

shaman: an Aboriginal spiritual leader

smudging: the act of burning sacred plants to cleanse people so that they can take part in the talking circle with honesty and a clear mind

Sovereign Council: a small group of people, including the governor, intendant, and bishop, that the French king appointed to govern the settlement in New France

Speaker's mace: a shaft that is decorated and is a symbol of the Speaker's power in a legislative assembly

special committee: a committee created to study a single issue or project, such as building a bridge

standing committee: a small group of people that meets regularly to discuss a particular area of community services

T

tax: money that is paid to the government

Territorial Commissioner: the monarch's representative in the territories

treaty: a formal agreement between groups of people, such as the agreements signed between First Nations peoples and the Canadian government

V

voyageur: a fur trader in New France with a licence to travel to meet and trade directly with First Nations peoples

W

wampum: beads made from shell that are strung together in patterns to make belts

wigwam: a dome- or cone-shaped structure made with a wooden frame that was covered with animal skins or tree bark

Index

Aboriginal peoples/rights, 12, 66–67, 89, 92, 179
Acadia, 179–181
Action plan, creating an, 98–99
Active citizens/citizenship, 4, 10, 13, 15, 86, 92, 93, 96, 101, 105
Acts, 42, 48–49, 87, 88–89
Algonkin, 116, 125, 127, 172, 182, 196
Alliances, 128, 129–131, 172–173, 182, 193, 196
Allies, 128, 131
Anishinabe, 82, 114–116, 118, 121, 125
Arctic sovereignty, 64–65
Artifacts, 65, 113, 117, 127, 129, 139–140
Assembly of First Nations, 66, 70, 80, 95

Band councils, 28–29, 80–81
Bartering, 161
Beavers, 165, 174–175
Beothuk, 157
Bills, 42, 48–49, 58
Boards, 20–21, 28
Brébeuf, Jean de, 186, 189–190, 193
British, 42, 56, 87, 92, 165
   See also English, The
Brûlé, Étienne, 143, 146
Budgets, 25, 47, 52, 62
By-elections, 38
Bylaws, 17, 24–25

Cabinet ministers, 40–41, 57
Cabinets, 40–41, 56–57
Cabot, John, 142, 149, 157
Canadian Charter of Rights and Freedoms, 88–89, 96
Canadian Citizenship Act, 87
Canadian Constitution, 55, 66–67, 74, 89
Candidates, 30, 38, 41, 61, 97

Cartier, Jacques, 143, 145, 147, 149, 150–153, 157
Champlain, Samuel de, 143, 146, 168–169, 172, 180, 182–183
Charter, Royal, 162
Chief, 21, 28, 49, 59, 66, 95, 121, 131, 145, 149–150, 153, 157, 162–163, 181, 192, 198
Chouart des Groseilliers, Médard, 165–166
Citizens, 10, 17, 23, 27, 30–31, 38, 43, 52, 54, 70–71, 77, 80, 86–87, 90–94, 96–97, 99–102, 104
Citizenship, 10, 14–15, 62, 87, 90–93, 97, 101, 105
Clan Mothers, 121, 131
Clans, 121, 131, 172
Clothing, 113–114, 116, 120–121, 123, 158, 187
Colonies, 135, 164, 180, 182–183, 188
Colonization, 138, 148
Commissions 21
Committees, 20–21, 28, 42, 93
Communication, 30–31, 34, 119, 151
Competitions, 128, 158, 166–167, 171, 174, 177, 181
Conclusions, draw 90–91, 101, 104, 111, 147, 185, 194–195, 199, 200, 204–205
Conflicts
   between different First Nations, 128–129, 130, 139, 193
   and First Nations land claims, 197
   between First Nations and Europeans, 139, 148–151, 157, 172–173, 192
   between France and England, 165, 167, 181
   between the Wendat and Jesuit missionaries, 192–193

Consensus governments, 41
Constitution Act, 88–89
Contact
   between First Nations and Europeans, 134, 139, 145–147, 148–149, 172–173
   between Inuit and Europeans, 151
   between the Wendat and Jesuit missionaries, 192–193
Councillors, 20, 22, 26, 27, 28
Coureurs de bois, 164, 165
Court of Appeal, 43
Court of Justice, 43

Decision making, 22, 119, 121, 123
De Monts, Pierre Du Gua, 180–181
Diseases, 150, 157, 173, 192–193, 194
Donnacona, Chief, 149, 150, 153

Eastern Canada
   European explorers in, 108–109, 135–137, 138–141, 142–143, 144
   and First Nations, 108–131
   fur trade in, 156–161, 164–167, 170–173
Education, 14, 29, 44, 45, 47, 66, 86
   minister of, 40
Elders, 113, 117, 124
Elections, 30–31, 37–38, 47, 60–61, 88, 92, 96–97
English, The
   explorers, 108–109, 142, 144
   and First Nations, 145, 149, 172–173, 181, 193, 196–197
   and the French, 167, 181
   and the fur trade, 157–158, 165–166, 171
   and Inuit, 151, 162
Environment, 13, 24–25, 48,

80–81, 82–83, 93, 114–116, 174, 192
  ministry of, 46, 59, 75
  patron saint of, 192
Eriksson, Leif, 138
European explorers
  in eastern Canada, 135–137, 142–143
  and First Nations, 108–109, 145–150
  and Inuit, 151
  land claims, 148
  the Norse, 138–141
  in northeastern Canada, 144
Europeans
  and First Nations, 108–111, 170, 172–173, 193, 196–197
  and fur trade, 158–159, 165–166, 170
Exchange of goods, 145, 148
Executive branch, 56, 57
Expeditions, 134, 135, 143
Explorations, 135–137, 142–144, 157, 174
Exploration routes, 138, 142–144

Far North Act, 48–49
Fashion (and the fur trade), 158, 175
Federal Court of Canada, 59
Federal government
  and Aboriginal peoples, 28–29, 66–67
  defined, 12–13, 55
  and homelessness, 77
  and law enforcement, 75
  and laws, 43
  members of, 60–61
  and natural disasters, 76
  natural resources, management by, 46
  and provinces and territories, 44, 47
  services of, 54, 62–63, 64–65
  structure of, 56–59
  and transportation, 74
Federal political parties, 61
Federation, 55
Filles du roi, 188

First Nations
  alliances, 128, 129–131, 172–173
  artifacts, 113, 116, 125, 129
  band councils, 28–29
  beliefs, 124–126, 189, 192
  children, 118
  clans, 121, 131
  clothing, 113–114, 116, 120–121, 123
  conflicts, 128, 139, 148–151, 171–173, 193
  consensus government, 41
  decision making, 119, 121, 131
  and diseases, 173
  education, 29, 66, 86
  Elders, 113, 117
  and the environment, 48–49, 89, 120, 114–116, 146–148, 175
  in Europe, 150
  and Europeans, 108–111, 139, 145–150, 154
  and *Far North Act*, 48–49
  food, 115, 117, 118, 120, 147
  and fur trade, 158–159, 160–161, 165–167, 170–171, 182
  interactions with each other, 117–119, 121, 123, 128–131, 171, 193
  and land claims, 148–149, 171, 197
  in L'Anse aux Meadows, 139–140
  locations on map, 48, 106–107, 114, 130
  men, 117, 131, 160
  and missionaries, 189
  oral tradition, 113
  petroglyphs, 127
  representation, 66–67
  rights of, 48–49, 66, 80, 86, 89, 154, 166, 171, 175, 179, 189, 196–197, 198
  roles of community members, 117–118, 131, 132, 160–161
  shelter, 115–116, 121
  spirituality, 119, 124–125, 189
  talking circles, 119
  technology, 146, 160
  trade with each other, 128, 157
  trade with Europeans, 139, 145, 157, 170
  treaties, 89, 196
  and voting, 60
  and water, 80
  women, 118, 131, 161, 173, 187
First readings, 42
Five nations, 130, 131
  See also Six Nations and Haudenosaunee
Fontaine, Phil, 95
Food, 46, 79, 84, 100, 114–115, 117–118, 120, 122, 124, 145, 147, 161, 182, 187, 191
Freedoms, 87, 88
French, The
  See also New France
  and English, 165–167, 172, 181
  explorers, 108–109, 143
  and First Nations, 109, 145, 146–147, 149, 164, 166–167, 172–173, 192–193, 196–197
  and fur trade, 158, 164–167
  settlements, 164, 179–190
Frobisher, Martin, 108, 144, 151
Fur trade
  See also Trade
  and Acadia, 180–181
  and the beaver, 174–175
  development of, 164–167
  and European goods, 170
  and clothing/fashion, 158, 160, 163, 177
  and First Nations, 158–159, 160–161, 165–167, 170–173
  and The Hudson's Bay Company, 166–167
  and Québec, 182–183
  start of, 157–159
  values of, 159

Geographical knowledge, 146
Government actions, 26–27, 41
Government
  See also Consensus government; Federal

government; Local governments; Municipal governments; Provincial governments; Territorial governments
   defined, 12–13, 57
   and the environment, 80–81
   and homelessness, 77
   and law enforcement, 75
   and natural disasters, 76
   in New France, 188
   and opposition, 39
   and people in need, 76–77
   and transportation, 74
   working together, 72–77, 80–85
Governor general, 56–57, 91, 198
Grand Council, 131
Great Lakes, 82–83, 115, 143
Great Law of Peace, 108, 112, 130, 196
Great Peace of Montréal, 109, 172, 196
Great Peacemaker, 130, 131
Great Spirit, 124

Habitants, 185
Hansard, 39, 40
Haudenosaunee, 112, 114–115, 118, 128–129, 172, 185, 191, 193–194, 200
   confederacy, 130–131, 196
Head of councils, 20–21
Healthcare, 13, 36, 44, 66, 78
Herjólfsson, Bjarni, 138
Hiawatha, 130
Hochelaga, 143, 145, 183
Homelessness, 76, 77, 84
House of Commons, 56, 58, 61
Hudson, Henry, 109, 144
Hudson Bay, 165–166, 171,
Hudson's Bay Company, 109, 162, 166
Huron, 190–191, 193–194
   See also Wendat

Île Sainte-Croix, 180
Information
   gather and organize, 68–69, 103, 152–153, 201
   interpret and analyze, 78–79, 162–163
Ingstad, Anne Stine, 140
Ingstad, Helge, 140
Innu, 116, 122–123, 139, 162, 172, 182, 189
Intendants, 188
Internet search tips, 152
Inuit, 12, 41, 45, 60, 64–65, 66–67, 108, 144, 151
Inuit Tapiriit Kanatami (ITK), 67

Jesuits, 125, 189, 190–193
Jikonsaseh, 130
Judicial branch, 56, 59
Jurisdiction, 17, 66, 75
Jorundardaughter, Thjodhild, 138

Kinship, 117
Kogawa, Joy, 95
Kowaluk, Lucia, 95

Land claims, 148–149, 171, 196–197
L'Anse aux Meadows, 138, 139–141
Law enforcement, 75
Laws, 12, 15, 17, 23, 37, 42–43, 56–59, 73, 87–88, 91, 175
   See also bylaws
   transportation laws, 74
   environmental laws, 75
Leader of the Official Opposition, 39–40, 58
Legislative assembly, 37, 41
Legislative branch, 56–58
Legislature, 37–42
Lieutenant Governors, 42
Local councils, 20–22, 30
Local governments
   See also Municipal governments
   band councils, 28
   bylaws, 24
   and communication, 30–31
   defined, 12–13, 17
   and municipalities, 18
   and other governments, 77
   services, 23
Longhouses, 115, 116, 121, 131, 191

Maps, analyzing, 50–51
   analyzing historical, 168
Mance, Jeanne, 183
Mayors, 20
Measles, 173, 192
Medicine, 44,
   First Nations, 114, 119, 146–147, 161, 187
Members of the provincial Parliament (MPPs), 37, 49, 105
Members of Parliament (MPs), 57, 58, 60–61, 105
Merchants, 158, 165, 170
Métis, 12, 36, 66, 67, 89, 173
Métis National Council (MNC), 67
Migrant workers, 55
Mi'kmaq, 116, 117, 124, 127, 131, 139, 142, 144, 152, 157, 163, 170, 174, 180–181, 189
Ministry
   of Agriculture and Food, 46
   of Education, 45
   of Natural Resources, 46, 83
   of Northern Development and Mines, 46
   of Environment, the, 46, 59
Missionary, 109, 179, 189, 190–193, 197
Missions, 190–194
Mohawk, 130–131, 192, 197
Monarch, 42, 56, 87
Montréal, 145, 176
   Great Peace of, 109, 172
Municipal
   council, 20, 22, 29
   department, 21
Municipal governments
   See also Local governments
   budget, 25
   communication and technology, 31

defined, 18
and homelessness, 77
and law enforcement, 75
and natural disasters, 76
and Ontario water treatment, 80
and provinces and territories, 19
structure of, 20–21
and the Toronto Zoo, 26
and transportation, 74
working with other levels of government, 73
Municipalities, 18–19, 23–25, 28–29, 32

Natural disasters, 76
Natural resources, management of, 44, 46, 49, 62, 83
Navigation, 137
New France
children in, 187
coureurs de bois, 164, 165
daily life in, 186–187t
and fur trade, 164–165
government of, 188
land division and development, 184–185, 197
men in, 186
missionaries in, 189
seigneurial system, 184–185
seigneurs, 184–185
seigneury, 184–185
settlements in, 179–183
timeline of, 108–109
and treaties, 196
voyageurs, 166–167, 173
women in, 187, 188
Norse, 138–141
See also Vikings
Nuns, 183, 189

Official Opposition, 39–40, 58, 61
Opposition
critics, 40
parties, 39–40, 58
Oral traditions, 113, 116, 142, 152–153

Order of Canada, 94–95

Parliament, 56–58, 60
buildings, 12
Parliament Hill, 54
Provincial Parliament, 37
Party system, 38, 41
Platform, 38
Police, 19, 23, 25, 75–76
North West Mounted Police, 62
Royal Ontario Mounted Police, 62, 75
Ontario Provincial Police, 83
Political parties, 38, 47, 61
Pollution, 32–34, 46, 81–82, 115
Port Royal, 163, 170, 174, 179–182
Premiers, 39–41
Priests, 170, 189–190, 193, 195
Prime minister, 56–58, 90
Protests, 10, 26, 30–31, 52, 63, 77, 86, 89, 197
Provincial governments
See also Territorial governments
and Angel Foundation for Learning, 79
and band councils, 28
and beaver population, 175
cabinets, 40
defined, 12–13, 37
and federal government, 55–56, 73
and homelessness, 77
and law enforcement, 75
and laws, 42–43
and local governments, 18–19
and natural disasters, 76
and opposition, 39
party system, 38
services, 44–47
and the Supreme Court, 59
and transportation, 74
and water treatment, 80
Provincial Parliament, 37
See also Parliament

Québec, 182–183

Québec City, 147, 182
Question Period, 58
Questions, formulate, 32–33, 102, 126–127, 200

Radisson, Pierre-Esprit, 165
Reeves, 20
Referendum, 30–31
Refugees, 68
Regional chairs, 20
Regional municipalities, 18–20
Representation by population, 60
Representative democracy, 130
Ridings, 37–38, 41
Royal Assent, 42
Royal Canadian Mounted Police (RCMP), 62, 75
See also Police
Rupert's Land, 166167, 171

Sainte-Marie among the Hurons, 190–191, 193–195
Scurvy, 147, 180, 182
Seigneurial system, 184–185
Seigneurs, 184–185
Seigneury, 184–185
Senate, 56, 58
Senators, 58
Services, 13, 15, 73–74
and band councils, 28–29
of federal government, 57–59, 62–63, 66
of local government, 17–18, 21–25
paying for, 25, 29, 47
of provincial and territorial governments, 37, 44–47
Settlements, 64, 109–110, 136, 179–197
and Jacques Cartier, 143
L'Anse aux Meadows, 138–141
Port Royal, 163, 174
and trade, 164, 167, 171–173
Six Nations, 112, 129 130, 132
reserve, the, 28, 29
Smallpox, 173, 192
Sovereignty, 64–65
Speaker of the House, 39–41

Special committees, 21–22, 42
Stadacona, 143, 147, 149–151, 182
Standing committees, 21–22
Superior Court of Justice, 43
Supreme Court of Canada, 56, 59

Talon, Jean, 188
Taxes, 25, 29, 47, 90, 185
Technology, 31, 44, 47, 137 146
Territorial Commissioners, 42
Territorial governments
   See also Provincial governments
   and band councils, 28
   cabinets, 40
   and consensus government, 41
   defined, 12–13, 37
   and federal government, 55–56, 73
   and homelessness, 77
   and laws, 42–43
   and local governments, 18–19, 25, 73
   and opposition, 39
   party system, 38
   services, 44–47
Trade
   amongst First Nations, 113, 122, 128, 157
   and exploration, 135–136, 157
   between First Nations and Europeans, 145, 170, 181, 196
   between First Nations and Vikings, 139
   foreign trade, 62–63
Trading posts, 156, 159–160, 164, 166–167, 172–173, 182
Transportation, 21, 23–25, 62, 73–74, 82, 160–161
Treaties, 89, 109, 167, 171–172, 181, 196
Tribal councils, 12, 28–29

Vikings, 108, 135, 138–141, 144
Ville-Marie, 178, 183
Volunteers, 54, 65, 81, 84, 93, 100
Votes and voting
   for government 15, 17, 30–31, 38, 41, 61, 88, 92, 96–97, 100
   in government, 20–22, 27, 42, 58
Voyageurs, 166–167, 173

Wabanaki Confederacy, 131
Wampum, 108, 129
Wendat, 119, 146, 172, 182, 185, 190
   See also Huron
   clothing, 116, 121
   decision making, 121
   food, 120
   and Haudenosaunee, 128–130, 193
   and missionaries, 186, 189–195
   shelter, 115, 121
   and spirituality, 124–125
   and trade, 128, 160
Wigwams, 116, 123, 189
Wolastoqiyik, 115, 157

Credits and Sources

This page constitutes an extension of the copyright page. We have made every effort to trace the ownership of all copyrighted material and to secure permission from copyright holders. In the event of any question arising as to the use of any material, we will be pleased to make the necessary corrections in future printings. Thanks are due to the following authors, publishers, and agents for permission to use the material indicated.

Photos

2: (top) © Valentino Visentini/Alamy; (centre) THE CANADIAN PRESS/Darryl Dyck; (bottom) QMI Agency files **3:** (top) Library and Archives of Canada; (centre) © INTERFOTO/Alamy; (bottom) SF photo/Shutterstock.com **4:** Silia Photo/Shutterstock.com **5:** Photo by Colin McConnell/Toronto Star via Getty Images **10:** (top) © Jason Pineau/All Canada Photos/Glow Images; (center) The Canadian Press Images/Robin Rowland; (bottom) © Felix Choo/Alamy **11:** (top) Adrian Wyld/TCPI/The Canadian Press; (center) CP PHOTO/Andrew Vaughan; (bottom) CP PHOTO/Thunder Bay Chronicle-Journal/Jamie Smith **12:** (top) CP PHOTO/AP Photo/David Vincent; (bottom) © Russ Heinl/All Canada Photos/Glow Images **13:** (top) Fuse/Thinkstock; (bottom) Aaron Haupt/Photo Researchers/Getty Images **14:** David Starrett/Nelson Education Ltd **15:** (top left) Jonah Bettio/Nelson Education Ltd; (center right) Jeff Greenberg/Photolibrary/Getty Images **16:** (top) David Starrett/Nelson Education Ltd; (bottom) SF photo/Shutterstock.com **17:** (top left) © FS Photography/Alamy; (top right) © pierre rochon/Alamy; (bottom) Dugald Bremner Studio/Getty Images **18:** (top) © Jim West/Alamy; (bottom) Ron Watts/All Canada Photos/Getty Images **19:** © Valentino Visentini/Alamy **20:** Fred Lum/The Globe and Mail/CP Picture Archive **21:** Lisa F. Young/Shutterstock.com **22:** Tony Tremblay/E+/Getty Images **23:** (bottom left) © Gideon Mendel/Corbis; (bottom right) © Michael Wheatley/Alamy **24:** Piotr Wawrzyniuk/Shutterstock.com **25:** Coin image © 2014 Royal Canadian Mint. All rights reserved/Image de pièce © 2014 Monnaie royale canadienne. Tous droits reserves **26:** Karel Gallas/Shutterstock.com **27:** Margaret Whittaker/Associated Press **28:** Jonah Bettio/Nelson Education Ltd **29:** Jonah Bettio/Nelson Education Ltd **30:** (top) yelo34/iStock/Thinkstock; (bottom) Pat McGrath/Ottawa Citizen. Reprinted by permission **32:** Toronto Star/GetStock.com **33:** The Canadian Press Images/Francis Vachon **34:** (top) David Starrett/Nelson Education Ltd; (bottom) © Performance Image/Alamy **36:** (top) Jonah Bettio/Nelson Education Ltd; (bottom) John Francis **37:** Perennial Foodie Traveler/Shutterstock.com **38:** (top) Errol McGihon/Ottawa Sun/QMI Agency; (center) Andy Clark/Reuters/Landov; (bottom) © Mark Spowart/Alamy **39:** Tim Krochak/Chronicle Herald, republished with permission from The Halifax Herald Ltd **40:** QMI Agency files **41:** (top) CP PHOTO/Kevin Frayer; (bottom) © Cindy Hopkins/Alamy **43:** Dick Hemingway **44:** The Globe and Mail/The Canadian Press **45:** (top) Photo by Colin McConnell/Toronto Star via Getty Images; (bottom) Carlos Osorio/GetStock.com **46:** Henry Georgi/All Canada Photos/Getty Images **47:** Coin image © 2014 Royal Canadian Mint. All rights reserved/Image de pièce © 2014 Monnaie royale canadienne. Tous droits reserves **48:** (top) Andrew McLachlan/Glow Images; (bottom) iStock/Thinkstock **49:** (top) © Yvette Cardozo/Alamy; (bottom) iStock/Thinkstock **52:** (top) Jonah Bettio/Nelson Education Ltd; (bottom) Veronica Henri/Toronto Sun/QMI Agency **54:** (top) David Starrett/Nelson Education Ltd; (bottom) Jupiterimages/Thinkstock **55:** © Lloyd Sutton/Alamy **56:** THE CANADIAN PRESS/AP Photo/David Cheskin, Pool **57:** National Geographic/Getty Images **58:** (top) THE CANADIAN PRESS/Sean Kilpatrick; (bottom) © Jack Fletcher/National Geographic Society/Corbis **59:** (top) Blair Gable/Reuters/Landov; (bottom) © Mark Bradley/All Canada Photos/Corbis **61:** (top to bottom) Reprinted by permission of the

Conservative Party of Canada; Reprinted by permission of the NDP; Reprinted by permission of the Liberal Party of Canada; Reprinted by permission of the Bloc Québécois Party; Reprinted by permission of the Green Party of Canada; Reprinted by permission of Parti Rhinoceros Party **62:** (top) © Radius Images/Glow Images; (bottom left) THE CANADIAN PRESS/Andrew Vaughan; (bottom right) Greg Biss/Glow Images; Bank note image used with the permission of the Bank of Canada **63:** (top left) Photo by Corporal Owen W. Budge, 8 Wing Imaging © 2013 DND-MDN Canada; (top right) THE CANADIAN PRESS/AP Photo/Jacquelyn Martin; (center) © Alex Stojanov/Alamy; (bottom) Rafael Ramirez Lee/Shutterstock.com **64:** © Yvette Cardozo/Alamy **65:** (top left) © Imagestate Media Partners Limited - Impact Photos/Alamy; (top center) Photo by: Cpl Aydyn Neifer, CFJIC High Readiness, © 2013 DND-MDN Canada; (top right) THE CANADIAN PRESS/Jonathan Hayward; (bottom) © Radius Images/Alamy **66:** © Jeff Vinnick **69:** © Michael Schmeling/Alamy **70:** (top) David Starrett/Nelson Education Ltd; (bottom) THE CANADIAN PRESS/Pawel Dwulit **72:** (top) David Starrett/Nelson Education Ltd; (bottom) Yellow Dog Productions/Stone/Getty Images **73:** (top) AFP/Getty Images; (bottom) THE CANADIAN PRESS/Darryl Dyck **74:** (top) © Roderick Paul Walker/Alamy; (bottom) Rev40, licensed under the Creative Commons Attribution-Share Alike 3.0 Unported license. **75:** Canada Border Services Agency **76:** (top) © TODD KOROL/Reuters/Corbis; (bottom) © MIKE STURK/Reuters/Corbis **77:** CP PHOTO/Edmonton Journal - John Lucas **80:** Tanya Talaga/GetStock.com **81:** (top) Rick Eglinton/Toronto Star/ZUMA Press/Newscom; (bottom) Design Pics/Peter Mather/Newscom **82:** Brian Hughes/GetStock.com **83:** (top) PHOTO FUN/Shutterstock.com; (bottom) CP PHOTO/AP Photo/John Flesher **84:** (top) David Starrett/Nelson Education Ltd; (bottom) Rae Holtsbaum/Winnipeg Sun/QMI Agency **86:** (top) David Starrett/Nelson Education Ltd; (bottom) THE CANADIAN PRESS/Sean Kilpatrick **87:** © Paul McKinnon/Alamy **88:** CP PHOTO **89:** (top right) monkeybusinessimages/iStock/Thinkstock; (bottom left) © Douglas MacLellan/Demotix/Corbis **90:** Tim Van Horn **91:** © Daniel Morel/Reuters/Corbis **92:** Boomer Jerritt/All Canada Photos/Glow Images **93:** (center left) Robert Tinker/First Light/Glow Images; (bottom center) Thomas Kitchin & Victoria Hurst/First Light/Glow Images **94:** (all) Office of the Governor General **95:** (top left) John Mahoney, The Gazette; (center right) Photo by Fred Lum/The Globe and Mail Digital Image/CP Picture Archive; (bottom left) Marcel Cretain/Winnipeg Sun/QMI Agency **96:** (center left) THE CANADIAN PRESS/Chris Young; (center right) David Starrett/Nelson Education Ltd; (bottom) THE CANADIAN PRESS/Adrian Wyld **97:** CP PHOTO/Dave Chidley **98:** Toronto Star via Getty Images **100:** (top) David Starrett/Nelson Education Ltd; (bottom) Toronto Star/GetStock.com **102:** © MBI/Alamy **103:** Comstock/Stockbye/Thinkstock **104:** monkeybusinessimages/iStock/Thinkstock **105:** © JLP/Jose L. Pelaez/Corbis **106:** (top) © Christopher Morris/Corbis; (bottom) © GraphicaArtis/Corbis **107:** (center left) © Francis Back; (center right) © Blue Lantern Studio/Corbis **108:** Popular Science Monthly Volume 28 **109:** (top left) Library and Archives Canada, Acc. No. R9266-1942 Peter Winkworth Collection of Canadiana; (top right) rook76/Shutterstock.com **110:** (center) RTimages/Shutterstock.com; (bottom) David Starrett/Nelson Education Ltd **111:** (top) Jonah Bettio; (center) © Design Pics Inc./Alamy **112:** (top) Jonah Bettio/Nelson Education Ltd; (bottom) Kara Wilson/Brantford Expositor/QMI Agency **113:** (left) Purchase from Mr. John H. Crouse, M13482, © McCord Museum; (right) Speniks lake objects, Canadian Museum of History, IMG2008-0007-1928-Dm **115:** (center right) © Paul Chesley/National Geographic Society/Corbis; (bottom) SF photo/Shutterstock.com **116:** (top left) Nativestock.com/Marilyn Angel Wynn/Getty Images; (center) With permission of the Royal Ontario Museum © ROM; (bottom left) Gift of Miss Anne McCord, ME982X.519.1-2, © McCord Museum **117:** (top right) Reprinted by permission of Hambleton Galleries; (bottom) © Danita Delimont/Alamy **118:** (top left) DEA/M. Seemuller/Getty Images; (centre) Reprinted by permission of Hambleton Galleries **119:** The Canadian Press Images/Francis Vachon **120:** Source: Library and Archives Canada/Credit: Charles William Jefferys/ William Jefferys fonds/C-069767 **122:** Gift of Mrs. W. D. Lighthall, M6016, © McCord Museum **124:** Seven Grandfather Teachings by Melissa Muir, Darla Martens-Reece, and Scott

Sampson, used with the kind permission of Melissa Muir **125:** (center left) AFP/Getty Images; (center right) With permission of the Royal Ontario Museum © ROM **127:** (top left and right) Bill Brooks/Masterfile; (bottom) © Parks Canada **128:** © Tom Till/Alamy **129:** Jonah Bettio/Nelson Education Ltd **130:** Drawing #171 Tree of Peace by John Fadden, reprinted with permission of the artist **132:** (top) Jonah Bettio/Nelson Education Ltd; (bottom) © Andrzej Bajer/Demotix/Corbis **134:** (top) David Starrett/Nelson Education Ltd; (bottom) RuthChoi/Shutterstock.com **136:** (top to bottom) Mirabelle Pictures/Shutterstock.com; Steven Prorak/iStock/Thinkstock; © Dorling Kindersley/Alamy; LiliGraphie/Shutterstock.com; Clive Mason/Getty Images **137:** (left and right) © INTERFOTO/Alamy **139:** Silia Photo/Shutterstock.com **140:** (top right) Parks Canada, G. Vandervloogt; (top center) Emory Kristof/National Geographic/Getty Images; (top right) © PF-(bygone1)/Alamy; (center right) Parks Canada Archaeology Lab, Reference 4A600A1-76; (bottom right) B. Wallace, Parks Canada **141:** (top) © James Steeves/Alamy; (center left) © James Steeves/Alamy **142:** (bottom left) © Image Asset Management Ltd/Alamy; (bottom center) Globe Turner/Shutterstock.com **143:** (top center) Stock Montage/Getty Images; (top right) Piotr Krzeslak/Shutterstock.com; (bottom center) © North Wind/North Wind Picture Archives **144:** (top) © INTERFOTO/Alamy; (bottom) © North Wind /North Wind Picture Archives **145:** Source: Library and Archives Canada/Peter Winkworth Collection of Canadiana at the National Archives of Canada/e002140173 **146:** Source: Library and Archives Canada/Credit: Charles William Jefferys/ Canadian Historical Paintings 1534-1884 collection. Thomas Nelson & sons/e008439701 **147:** Source: Library and Archives Canada/ Peter Winkworth Collection of Canadiana at the National Archives of Canada/e002140173 **149:** Gift of Confederation Life Association, M976.179.1, © McCord Museum **150:** Gaspé on Friday, July 24, 1534, painted by Francis Back, Canadian Museum of History, IMG2011-0156-0007-Dm **151:** © The Print Collector/Corbis **152:** Source: Library and Archives Canada/Credit: Charles William Jefferys/Canadian Historical Paintings 1534–1884 collection. Thomas Nelson & sons/c013985 **154:** (top) David Starrett/Nelson Education Ltd; (bottom) THE CANADIAN PRESS/Darryl Dyck **156:** (top) Sanmongkhol/Shutterstock.com; (bottom) Time & Life Pictures/Getty Images **157:** (left) Library and Archives Canada, nlc-8713; (right) Library and Archives Canada/C-038862 **158:** Hudson's Bay Company Archives, Archives of Manitoba, 1987/363-C-308, N8318 **160:** © Prisma Bildagentur AG/Alamy **161:** Library and Archives Canada, C-069576 **162:** Hudson's Bay Company Archives, Archives of Manitoba, PAM P-385 (N9033), HBC's 1921 calendar illustration **163:** Library and Archives of Canada **164:** Library and Archives Canada/C-073423 **165:** © Corbis **167:** (top left) Library and Archives Canada/C-008373; (bottom right) © Terrance Klassen/Alamy **168:** Library and Archives Canada, MIKAN no. 4153517 **169:** Debra Lackas/Thinkstock **170:** National Gallery of Canada (no. 6663) **171:** HBC Corporate Collection **172:** (center left) © CORBIS; (bottom right) Numérisation et collage de 3 pages du livre : La Grande Paix, Chronique d'une saga diplomatique, Alain Beaulieu, Montréal, éditions Libre Expression, 2001 **173:** CP PHOTO/Winnipeg Free Press - Jeff de Booy **174:** © Marshall Ikonography/Alamy **176:** (top) Sanmongkhol/Shutterstock.com; (bottom) Library and Archives Canada/C-011013 **178:** (top) © moodboard/Corbis; (bottom) © Francis Back **180:** Library and Archives Canada/e010764741 **181:** (top) Copyright: Canada Post Corporation Credit: Library and Archives Canada/MIKAN 3725109; (bottom) Alan Syliboy, Painting of Chief Membertou, © CARCC, 2014 **182:** (left) Library and Archives Canada; (right) Russ Heinl/All Canada Photos/Getty Images **183:** (left) Library and Archives Canada, Acc. No. 1984-164-91 Source: Mr. Laurent Allard, Laval, Québec; (right) Vrai Portrait de Marguerite Bourgeoys, Pierre Le Ber, Collection of the Congrégation de Notre-Dame, Marguerite Bourgeoys Museum **184:** Russ Heinl/All Canada Photos/Getty Images **185:** Library and Archives Canada/nlc-8902 **186:** Getty Images **187:** Library and Archives Canada, Acc. No. 1983-45-3/C-011925 **188:** Library and Archives Canada, Acc. no. 1996-371-1 **189:** Library and Archives Canada, Acc. No. 1983-45-1/C-010520 **190:** Photo courtesy of Sainte-Marie among the Hurons, Midland, Ontario, Canada **191:** © Arco Images/Glow Images **192:** (center left) © Robert Mayne USA/Alamy; (bottom) © Marilyn

Angel Wynn/Nativestock Pictures/Corbis **193:** (top right) Donald Ford/iStock/Thinkstock; (center) © Hemis/Alamy **194:** Gift of Confederation Life Association, M976.180.3, © McCord Museum **196:** CP PHOTO/La Presse-Robert Skinner **197:** THE CANADIAN PRESS/Shaney Komulainen **198:** (top) © moodboard/Corbis; (bottom) THE CANADIAN PRESS/Fred Chartrand **200:** Photo courtesy of Sainte-Marie among the Hurons, Midland, Ontario, Canada **202:** © moodboard/Corbis **203:** © Blend Images/Alamy

Text

10: Reprinted with permission of Catholic Online www.catholic.org **16, 35, 36, 53, 54, 71, 122, 178, 179, 199:** [Scripture quotations are from] The New Revised Standard Version (Anglicized Edition), copyright 1989, 1995 by the Division of Christian Education of the National Council of the Churches of Christ in the United States of America. Used by permission. All rights reserved. **25:** Data from Statistics Canada, CANSIM table 385-0024. **26:** Quotation beginning "Please I would like to ask all those who have positions…" from Homily of Pope Francis, Saint Peter's Square, Tuesday, 19 March 2013 http://www.vatican.va/holy_father/francesco/homilies/2013/documents/papa-francesco_20130319_omelia-inizio-pontificato_en.html . Libreria Editrice Vaticana **28:** The map of the Ogemawahj Tribal Council has been adapted from the map on the tribal council's website. **32–33:** Quotes appeared in a Toronto Star article, "Landfill or incinerator: What's the future of Toronto's trash?" by Alyshah Hasham, March 12, 2013, http://www.thestar.com/news/gta/2013/03/12/landfill_or_incinerator_whats_the_future_of_torontos_trash.html **37:** Elections Ontario, http://www.cpcml.ca/images2011/Provinces/Ontario/2011OntarioElectionResultsCombined.jpg **39:** Saint John Paul, Ecclesia in America, no. 44, http://www.vatican.va/holy_father/john_paul_ii/apost_exhortations/documents/hf_jp-ii_exh_22011999_ecclesia-in-america_en.html **46:** Pope Benedict XVI, Caritas in Veritate, no. 48, http://www.vatican.va/holy_father/benedict_xvi/encyclicals/documents/hf_ben-xvi_enc_20090629_caritas-in-veritate_en.html **47:** Five Largest Areas of Expense in the Ontario Budget for 2013-2014 from 2013 Ontario Budget Chapter II: Ontario's Economic Outlook and Fiscal Plan, Section G: Details of Ontario's Finances, TABLE 2.24 Total Expense. Queen's Printer for Ontario. **49:** (top) Speech by Michael Gravelle, former Minister of Natural Resources, Ontario, as appearing in http://www.netnewsledger.com/2011/12/01/viewpoint-the-far-north-act-michael-gravelle-mpp/; (center) Stan Beardy, Grand Chief, Nishnawbe Aski Nation, as quoted in "NAN goes on offensive to fight Bill 191" by Rick Garrick, Wawatay News, September 1, 2010, http://wawataynews.ca/archive/all/2010/9/1/nan-goes-offensive-fight-bill-191_20268. This quote also appears in other publications, including "NAN launches campaign against Far North Act," The Daily Press, August 1, 2010, http://www.timminspress.com/2010/08/31/nan-launches-campaign-against-far-north-act/; (bottom left) Speech by Norm Miller, MPP, Parry Sound-Muskoka, http://www.netnewsledger.com/2012/03/23/norm-miller-on-far-north-act/; (bottom right) Julie Denomme, vice chair, Greater Sudbury Chamber of Commerce, as appearing in "More questions than answers in Far North Act," September 10, 2011, Sudbury Star **51:** Figures on family doctors came from Statistics Canada 2011 Household Survey: Data Tables -- the writers compiled the information by selecting each province/territory to find out what the figures were for #3112 (GPs and FPs): http://www12.statcan.gc.ca/nhs-enm/2011/dp-pd/dt-td/Rp-eng.cfm?LANG=E&APATH=3&DETAIL=0&DIM=0&FL=A&FREE=0&GC=0&GID=0&GK=0&GRP=0&PID=105897&PRID=0&PTYPE=105277&S=0&SHOWALL=1&SUB=0&Temporal=2013&THEME=96&VID=0&VNAMEE=&VNAMEF=. The population estimates came from Statistics Canada, Census 2011, http://www12.statcan.ca/census-recensement/2011/dp-pd/hlt-fst/pd-pl/Table-Tableau.cfm?LANG=Eng&T=101&S=50&O=A. **68:** Citizenship and Immigration Canada, Facts and figures 2012 – Immigration overview: Permanent and temporary residents, Canada – Permanent residents by province or territory and urban area. Reproduced with the permission of the Minister of Public Works and Government Services Canada, 2014. **72, 85:** Gaudium Et Spes,, no. 25, http://www.vatican.va/archive/

hist_councils/ii_vatican_council/documents/vat-ii_cons_19651207_gaudium-et-spes_en.html **78:** Child poverty data is sourced from Statistics Canada, CANISM Table 202-0802, Persons in Low Income Families **82:** Adapted from Environment Canada , Cleaning Up the Great Lakes, map for the status of the Canadian areas of concern and updates on lake-wide management, http://www.ec.gc.ca/doc/eau-water/grandslacs-greatlakes_e.htm **86, 101:** Pope John XXIII, Peace on Earth, no. 26 **90:** (center left) John Diefenbaker, http://www.cic.gc.ca/english/resources/publications/discover/quotes.asp; (center right) Figure entitled What Makes Someone a Good Citizen. Information is from "Canadians On Citizenship-The First National Survey on What It Means to be a Citizen in Canada, Final Report, February 2012" found at The Institute for Canadian Citizenship, http://www.icc-icc.ca/en/news/docs/2012/Canadians%20on%20Citizenship%20-%20Final%20Report%20-%20Mar%201.pdf **91:** Citizenship and Immigration Canada, Discover Canada: The Rights and Responsibilities of Citizenship, © Her Majesty the Queen in Right of Canada, represented by the Minister of Citizenship and Immigration Canada, 2014 **92:** Citizenship and Immigration Canada, adapted from "Discover Canada: The Rights and Responsibilities of Citizenship," http://www.cic.gc.ca/english/resources/publications/discover/section-04.asp **97:** Taking Stock: An Examination of Conscience, October 10, 2007, page 3, Ontario Conference of Catholic Bishops, http://www.ccrl.ca/doc/TakingStock.pdf **100:** "The Common Good and the Catholic Church's Social Teaching" a statement by the Catholic Bishops' Conference of England and Wales, 1996, page 19, http://justice-and-peace.org.uk/documents/TheCommonGood.pdf **106:** Pope Paul VI, On The Development of Peoples, no. 43, http://www.papalencyclicals.net/Paul06/p6develo.htm **111:** Pope Paul VI, On The Development of Peoples, no. 43, http://www.papalencyclicals.net/Paul06/p6develo.htm **112, 133:** Source: Saint John XXIII **134, 155:** Saint John Paul II, http://www.vatican.va/holy_father/john_paul_ii/messages/peace/documents/hf_jp-ii_mes_19801208_xiv-world-day-for-peace_en.html **141:** Adapted map of L'Anse aux Meadows National Historic Site, © Parks Canada **148:** (top) Elder Twylah Hurd Nitsch, Seneca First Nation From In the Words of Elders: Aboriginal Cultures in Transition, by Peter Kulchyski. University of Toronto Press, 1999; (bottom left) Saskatchewan Social Studies 5 by Dana Antayá-Moore, et al., Pearson Education Canada 2013, page 281, and http://mettahu.wordpress.com/2013/07/17/worldview/ ;(bottom right) Saskatchewan Social Studies 5 by Dana Antayá-Moore, et al., Pearson Education Canada 2013, page 281, and http://mettahu.wordpress.com/2013/07/17/worldview/ **153:** Excerpt from Jacques Cartier's journal of 1534, translated by H.P. Biggar in The Voyages of Jacques Cartier, 1924 **156, 177:** Source: Pope Paul VI, On the Development of Peoples, no. 59, http://www.papalencyclicals.net/Paul06/p6develo.htm **157:** Excerpt from Jacques Cartier's journal of 1534, translated by H.P. Biggar in The Voyages of Jacques Cartier, 1924. **159:** (top right) The New Revised Standard Version (Anglicized Edition), copyright 1989, 1995 by the Division of Christian Education of the National Council of the Churches of Christ in the United States of America. Used by permission. All rights reserved; (bottom left) Illustration was created based on the following sources: www.canadiana.ca/hbc/stories/produits2_e.html. 1706 Standards of Trade; idea for illustration is from Canada Revised 6 by Arnold Gibbs, (c) 1999 Arnold Publishing Ltd., page 211 **162:** (bottom left) The Royal Charter for Incorporating The Hudson's Bay Company, 1670, https://archive.org/details/cihm_21022; (bottom right) Excerpt beginning "The beaver does everything well An Innu chief said to Father Paul Le Jeune"… from The Jesuit Relations and Allied Documents: Travels and Explorations of the Jesuit Missionaries in New France, 1610-1791, Volume 6, page 296, originally compiled and translated by Reuben Gold Thwaites in 1902 **175:** "Rethinking the beaver" by Frances Blackhouse, Canadian Geographic, December 2012, http://www.canadiangeographic.ca/magazine/dec12/beaver.asp - Map by Chris Brackley/Canadian Geographic **186:** Quote from Father Brebeuf beginning ""You note, in the first place…" appeared in The Jesuit Relations and Allied Documents: A Selection, edited by S.R. Mealing, McGill Queens University Press, December 1990 **189:** Quotation beginning "I am greatly astonished that the French…" from New Relation of Gaspesia by Chrestien Le Clercq, translated and edited by William F. Ganong, The Champlain Society, 1910, page 103.